The Deceivers

By the same author

THE HOLLOW CROWNS

A History of the Battles of the Wars of the Roses

The Deceivers

*"**Deceiver** : 1. One who makes [a person] believe
what is false; who misleads purposely.
2. One who is unfaithful."*
(O.E.D.)

The solution to the murder of the
Princes in the Tower

GEOFFREY RICHARDSON

Baildon Books, Shipley, England

First published 1997
Reprinted 2001

by Baildon Books
P.O. Box 107, SHIPLEY, W. Yorks BD17 6UR

Printed in Great Britain by
Think Ink
11-13 Philip Road, Ipswich, Suffolk, IP2 8BH
Tel: 01473 400162

ISBN 0 9527621 1 0

This book is for my dear niece, Brenda Skogg,
of Ocean Shores, Australia, and her father, my
older brother, Kenneth, without whose joint
encouragement, it would never have been written.
And ever and always for my lovely wife, Betty.

CONTENTS

Illustrations and Maps

Portraits of Edward IV, Richard III and Henry VII are reproduced by kind permission of the Society of Antiquaries of London. All other illustrations, Coats of Arms and signatures are provided by Geoffrey Wheeler of London. Original Battlemaps from "The Hollow Crowns" were drawn by Roy Barton, NDD, ATD.

The House of Plantagenet
Edward III
(1312 - 77)

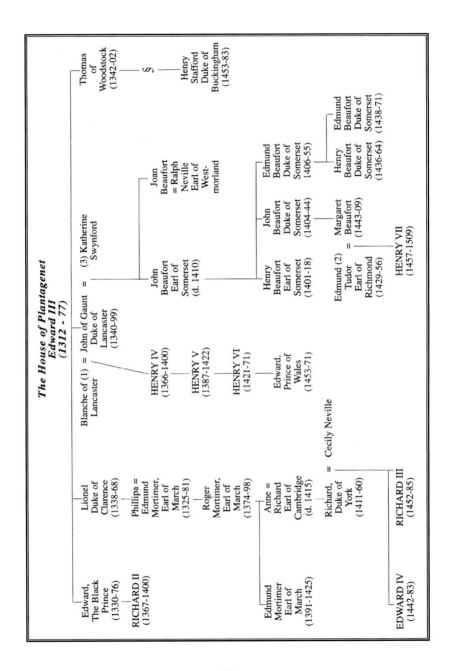

Edward III (1312-77) = (3) Katherine Swynford, and Blanche of (1) Lancaster = John of Gaunt Duke of Lancaster (1340-99)

Thomas of Woodstock (1342-02)
§
Henry Stafford Duke of Buckingham (1453-83)

Joan Beaufort = Ralph Neville Earl of Westmorland

John Beaufort Earl of Somerset (d. 1410)

Edmund Beaufort Duke of Somerset 1406-55
Henry Beaufort Duke of Somerset (1436-64)
Edmund Beaufort Duke of Somerset (1438-71)

John Beaufort Duke of Somerset (1404-44)
Margaret Beaufort (1443-09) = Edmund (2) Tudor Earl of Richmond (1429-56)
HENRY VII (1457-1509)

Henry Beaufort Earl of Somerset (1401-18)

HENRY IV (1366-1400)
HENRY V (1387-1422)
HENRY VI (1421-71)
Edward, Prince of Wales (1453-71)

Edward, The Black Prince (1330-76)
RICHARD II (1367-1400)

Lionel Duke of Clarence (1338-68)
Phillipa = Edmund Mortimer, Earl of March (1325-81)
Roger Mortimer, Earl of March (1374-98)
Edmund Mortimer Earl of March (1391-1425)
Anne = Richard Earl of Cambridge (d. 1415)

Richard, Duke of York (1411-60) = Cecily Neville
EDWARD IV (1442-83)
RICHARD III (1452-85)

10

PREFACE

Three years ago, being house-bound caring for my terminally-ill wife, I decided it would be good mental therapy to try to achieve a life-time's ambition and write The Definitive Military History of the Wars of the Roses. Somewhat to my surprise, I succeeded and "The Hollow Crowns" was published in August, 1996.

While researching the final two chapters of the book, dealing with the brief reign of Richard III and the Battle of Bosworth, I noticed - for the first time - that, following the execution of Lord Hastings, John Morton, Bishop of Ely, was placed in the custody of Henry Stafford, Duke of Buckingham, at the Duke's own request. And I asked myself, Why ? And one thought led to another until, quite suddenly, I knew why Hastings died as he did and - much more important - I realised who was really responsible for the murder of the Princes in the Tower. This Damascene Revelation - I can think of it in no other terms - left me in some difficulty. I had not set out to write a defence of Richard III when I started the book, though I had never believed him capable of killing his beloved brother's two sons, nor would such a digression fit logically into a military history of the period. On the other hand, what I had discovered (and felt had somehow been missed by all other historical writers) seemed too important to disregard and I therefore added it to the book as an Appendix titled "Who Killed the King ?"

After the launch of "The Hollow Crowns" I was encouraged to develop the Appendix into a separate book, and "The Deceivers" is the result. Readers will note my use of the plural noun which is made necessary by further discoveries as my research for the new history developed. In brief, I have come to believe that the deaths of the Princes in the Tower, of Lord Hastings and, effectively, of Buckingham and Richard III himself were brought about through the collective scheming of three people, who, to the best of my knowledge, have never previously been indicted for the crimes of which they are guilty.

The Wars of the Roses, as they were named centuries afterwards, lasted almost exactly 30 years. They consisted of 11 major battles - fought in two main clusters - starting with First St Albans on May 22nd, 1455 and ending at Bosworth on August 22nd, 1485. Some historians have argued that Stoke Field, fought on June 16, 1487 was, effectively, the last battle but apart from - and notably - John de Vere, Earl of Oxford, and a handful of survivors from Bosworth, few of the participants on either side at Stoke had any involvement in the earlier conflicts. There is little or no element of continuity, therefore, to link Stoke with the earlier fighting and most students of the period will continue to prefer August 22nd, 1485 as the last day of the Wars.

This History covers the last two years of the internecine struggle between the two Houses of Plantagenet, York and Lancaster, from the death of Edward IV in April 1483, through the defeat and death of his successor and youngest brother, Richard III at Bosworth in 1485 and the early years of the usurper, Henry Tudor, to the appearance of Perkin Warbeck, the last Yorkist pretender to Henry's throne. It sets out to answer a number of questions which had always puzzled me, and, it appears, many other students of that tumultuous half-century in our History when the Middle Ages ended and the Renaissance period began:

– Why was the life of the old Yorkist War-horse, William Hastings, ended so abruptly and so ingloriously -

– Why should Henry Stafford, second Duke of Buckingham, rebel against the King he had helped to his throne only three months earlier -

– How could a seasoned warrior like Richard III lose the Battle of Bosworth against what, at best, was little more than "a rabble in arms"-

and most mysterious of all:

– Who killed the Princes in the Tower - and When and Why ?

The answers to all these questions have, I believe, now appeared through careful assessment of the actions of a handful of people identified progressively as the investigation proceeded, who combined to change the pattern of English History. In the end, it has seemed to me that, in the words of the Bard, "The evil that men do lives after them, the good is oft interred with their bones..." or, to paraphrase Churchill: Never have so few exerted so much influence on the course of our island's story and to such malign effect.

Be that as it may, I have set down the truth of the matter as I have discovered it through long and detailed study of the key players in the story, whose locations at critical moments and physical involvement - direct or otherwise - in the events described are documented and vouched for, mainly in sources sympathetic to the real villains of the piece, those I have chosen to call "The Deceivers". All the sources used, and the information extrapolated from them, are listed in detailed Notes at the end of the narrative and I leave it to the reader to decide who has the right of it.

As I wrote in "The Hollow Crowns", if this new theory is accepted, a great wrong will have been righted. At worst, the entirely new line of thought presented may encourage others to look again into the mass of information which has been unearthed about what the American Historian, Paul Kendall has called "the most famous mystery in the annals of England", and produce the final answer to a question now more than 500 years old.

For me, the only continuing mystery is why it has taken so long to arrive at the real truth.

Edward IV

(Society of Artiquaries of London)

CHAPTER ONE

"...All of us have cause
To wail the dimming of our shining star..."

In his Palace of Westminster, the King was dying. The massive body was still now under the covers, the breathing stertorous, rasping in the inflamed lungs. The great bedchamber was quiet. The Lords and nobles had left after being reconciled to each other at the King's urging - the upstart Woodvilles led by the King's stepsons, Thomas Grey, Marquess of Dorset and his brother Lord Richard, whose father had died at Towton fighting for Lancaster, and the older nobility led by the King's most steadfast supporter Lord Hastings. The physicians had gone, there was no more for them to do. Only the priests were left, praying for the departing soul of England's greatest warrior King.

The life of Edward IV of the House of Plantagenet of York was all but over. He had ruled England for more than twenty years from a throne seized by force from the failing grasp of Henry VI, and held by the strength of his arms against all comers. Margaret of Anjou, Henry's Queen, who had died a poor pensioner of the Spider King, Louis of France; the mighty Nevilles led by Richard of Warwick and his brother John, Marquess Montagu, killed in a battle they could and should have won; the Cliffords and Dacres, hard northern Lords who paid for their allegiance to Lancaster with their lives; the Tudors and their Welshmen, dead or fled and, above all the Beauforts, the Somersets with their unending stream of armies from the Southwest - all had tried and failed to snatch the sceptre from Edward's mighty grasp.

But now, the victor of Northampton and Mortimer's Cross, the fighting general who held his line together through the blizzards of bloody Towton and who hammered out unlikely victories at Barnet and Tewkesbury had reached the end of his course. The giant six and a half foot frame which led the Yorkist armies like a living Fighting-man Standard against their Lancastrian foes had become gross in the soft living of the twelve years of peace Edward's victories had secured for England. With no more fields to conquer, he had given his time to feasting and lavish living and womanising and now the account for all was presented. The physicians diagnosed a "great catarrh", which medical experts in a later age would term bronchopneumonia and pleurisy. The name matters little. In an age centuries before the advent of antibiotics the patient would surely die.

What thoughts coursed through that fevered mind at the end ? Concern for his young sons Edward and Richard, named for himself and his youngest brother ? Would their lives be marred as his and Richard of Gloucester's had been by constant warring, plot and counterplot, conspiracy, tragedy, and treason ? No, surely not. Richard, named as Protector in his will would see to it that his son Edward's reign was soundly based until the boy was old enough to take matters into his own hands. Richard would ensure that the plotting of Louis, the wily French spider-king, who had broken the marriage compact between his son and Edward's lovely daughter, Elizabeth, a year before - and reneged on payment of the pension to the King of England - would come to naught.

And Lancaster - no cause for concern there. Edward had finally shattered the dreams of the usurpers 12 years before on a fine May morning by the Avon winding its lazy way past Tewkesbury in the west country. In three short weeks he had ended 20 long years of war and made his throne safe from the false claim of his cousins of Lancaster and from the vaunting ambition of the House of Neville. In his last moments, did Edward's greatest and final triumphs live again in his fevered mind ?

Remembering perhaps the thick early-morning mist that Easter Sunday - strange how Eastertide had always been lucky for him - his hard-fought victory at Towton, surely the greatest battle which would ever be fought in England, had been won on Palm Sunday. And now, on the anniversary of the Resurrection, with 10,000 men in three divisions, Hastings to the left, his brother Richard of Gloucester in his first command to the right, Edward probed blindly forward towards the waiting Lancastrian line at Barnet.

The coming battle was the climax to events since his return to England a month earlier, following a half-year exile at his brother-in-law's court in Burgundy. The ever-crafty Louis of France had earlier stitched together an 'impossible' alliance between Richard Neville, Earl of Warwick and Margaret of Anjou, Henry VI's Queen, when the irreconcilable pair, both fugitives from Edward's wrath, had taken refuge at the French court. Warwick had returned to England, found help from his brother John, Marquis Montagu and from Edward's brother George, Duke of Clarence and reinstalled the hapless Henry VI on the throne. Awaiting Margaret's return, he had been taken by surprise

BARNET. April 14th 1471. First Phase.

N

London and Barnet

HASTINGS

EDWARD

GLOUCESTER.

OXFORD

MONTAGUE

EXETER

Enfield

To St.Albans

HATFIELD

Wrotham Wood.

Hadley Wood.

BARNET. April 14th 1471. Second Phase.

by Edward's sudden landing at Ravenspur, and had set about gathering troops for the inevitable confrontation. But slowly, too slowly to prevent the Yorkist King from reaching his main power-base in London, where, joined again by Clarence, he assembled a new army to do battle with Lancaster and marched north to meet the approaching Warwick.

The uneasy alliance of Nevilles and Lancaster took their stand across a ridge, reputedly the highest such feature between York and London, to the north of a village called Barnet. Montagu commanded the centre, knowing that Edward himself was sure to be his opponent leading the Yorkist mainward, with the young de Vere, Earl of Oxford, Lancastrian firebrand flaunting his shooting star banners on the right and Exeter, former Admiral of England and an old opponent of Warwick, holding the Lancastrian left. Richard Neville, who would go down in history as "The Kingmaker", took his now customary position with the reserve division, where he could observe the battle's development - and keep well clear of any physical involvement.

The army of Lancaster held a strong position, with much of the centre and right protected by a hedge, and, with superior numbers, Warwick's strategy was to await the inevitable attack which he knew would come from his old pupils, Edward and Richard, and wear the Yorkists down in a slogging match. John de Vere, Earl of Oxford, however, had his own ideas and as the first tentative contacts came with Hastings' division, he urged his troops forward to the attack. King Edward had arrayed his army in the dark and was unaware that his force was placed too far to the right, nor, in the thick early mist of that Easter Day, did this error become quickly apparent. Thus, Oxford's men found they outflanked Hastings' troops, and the Yorkist left, finding themselves assailed front, flank and rear, broke and ran - some not staying for rest till they reached London again.

Now it was the mist that saved Edward. Neither general saw the flight of Hastings men and Edward fought grimly on in the centre against Montagu, while Exeter, finding his flank turned by the over-extended right of the Yorkists, was falling back and back, pressed by the eager Gloucester, and calling on Warwick for support from the reserve. Oxford, realising that the day was far from won, regathered his men from their looting of the Yorkist baggage train and turned back to attack the rear of Edward's central division, not knowing that the line of battle had swung through 90 degrees, so that his second valiant charge of the day struck not his hated Yorkist foes, but the right flank of Montagu's division. John Neville and his northerners finding themselves under continuing attack from their former Yorkist allies to the front, and mistaking de Vere's shooting star banner for Edward's own Sun with streamers sent volleys of arrows into the new onslaught, and the old, familiar cry of "Treachery, treachery" was raised by both divisions of Lancaster's army, which started to dissolve in confusion.

Edward, sensing the weakening of the front facing him so steadfastly till now and seeing Gloucester's strong advance on his right as the mist finally began to break, urged his men to still greater efforts and the army of the Nevilles, so nearly victorious an hour before, broke and fled. Montagu died in the front line of his division, Warwick's stripped corpse was found later, short of the succour of the horse-lines. Both bodies were taken back to London and displayed on the steps of St Paul's, so that all might see the end to which the once-mighty Earl of Warwick, ruler of England, maker of Kings, had come.

And now, with his breathing shorter, ever more-laboured, did great Edward fear his own approaching end ? Or was his mind still filled by the mighty efforts of the past, the swift march to the west country only days after Barnet had been won, as tidings reached him of a new threat from a returned Queen joined with the old foe, Somerset? Did he relive the race for the crossing of the Severn , where Margaret would find sure haven with Jasper Tudor and strong reinforcement from the Welshmen ? Did the roar of his last battle again fill the dying ears, the clangour of the final meeting when the last Lancastrian host was brought to bay, still short of their goal, that fine May morning in the Tewkesbury meadows ?

Both armies had rested the night before the fight. Sleep and rest were essential, for the Yorkist hounds had pursued the Vixen of Lancaster over 60 miles of twisting, dusty, westcountry lanes as she and her army made for their Welsh refuge. But, with safety across the Severn at last in sight, there was neither space nor time to cross, unless the King's army could be thrown back to give the few hours necessary to reach safety.

Edmund Beaufort, Duke of Somerset, commander of the Queen's army had grander ideas than winning a little more time to ensure safety in further flight. He rose early on the morning of May 4th, 1471 and rode out to survey the battleground. In front of his right wing was a small wooded knoll, which he saw would conceal a flanking movement aimed at Edward's left and any reduction of manpower in his right-hand division would be concealed from the Yorkists by broken ground and a hedged lane running across his front. Here lay the key to a stunning victory for Lancaster - a flank attack would shatter the usurping Edward's left and his whole array could be rolled up as the Lancastrian centre charged to reinforce the inevitable success of Somerset's surprise attack. Satisfied, the Duke returned to his camp to detail his strategy to Lord Wenlock and the young Prince of Wales, who would jointly command the centre division.

Unhappily for Somerset, he was opposed by a much more experienced general who had likewise risen early and surveyed the ground between the two armies. Edward surmised the main threat to his own force would be to his left flank and decided, against all tradition, to deploy his force by wheeling to the left into line, thus giving his younger brother, Richard of Gloucester,who was leading the vanguard, command of his left wing and Hastings, whose men had proved less reliable at Barnet, taking over the right flank. In addition, Edward would reinforce his left by concealing 200 mounted lances in a heavily wooded area beyond the knoll. Equally satisfied with his plans, the King returned to his quarters to arm himself for the fight.

About mid-morning, Edward brought his army forward from their overnight billets and arrayed his three divisions to match the Lancastrian dispositions opposite. The ground between the two was broken by hedges and ditches, which would make for problems in manoeuvring, but, eager to make a final reckoning with Lancaster, Edward signalled his brother to attack to his front and urged his own division forward towards the enemy centre, where the Prince of Wales Feathers flaunted in the Spring breeze.

Gloucester immediately set his own force in motion, moving slowly over the broken ground towards the hedge-hidden line where the Beaufort banners waved and received the full shock of Somerset's flanking charge as Lancaster's right wing broke from the cover of the hillock and flung themselves on their surprised opponents. Immediately, the men of York recoiled towards their centre, as Somerset expected, but the wing did not break. Edmund Beaufort had to deal with a different calibre of fighting general from that Oxford had found at Barnet and Richard held his line together and swung round, step by step, to face the threat from his left.

The Yorkists' wheel to their left necessarily exposed their right flank to an attack from Lancaster's centre, again as Somerset had anticipated, but Wenlock, one of the great coat-turners of the Wars of the Roses, made no move to his support. Somerset sent messengers urging Wenlock and the Prince to attack, while himself continuing to press Gloucester's wing backwards on to the Yorkist centre, when Edward's defensive foresight paid

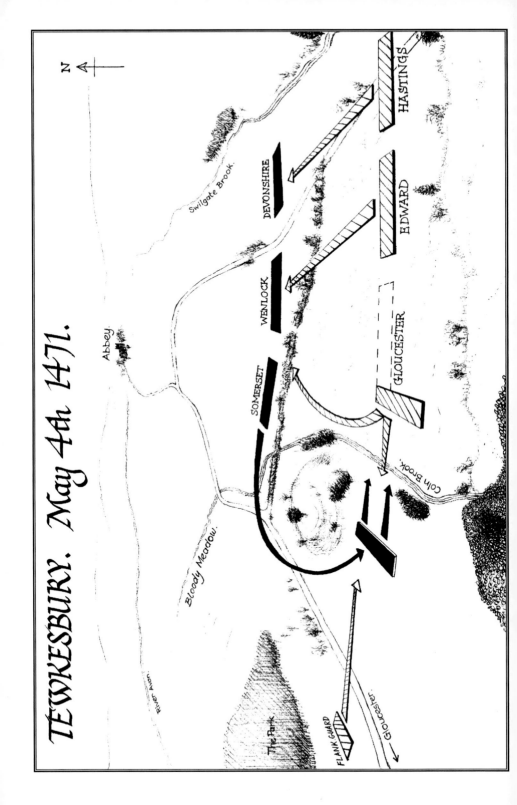

TEWKESBURY. May 4th 1471.

N

Abbey.

River Avon.

The Park.

Bloody Meadow.

Swilgate Brook.

Coln Brook.

Gloucester.

FLANK GUARD

GLOUCESTER

SOMERSET

WENLOCK

DEVONSHIRE

EDWARD

HASTINGS

unexpected dividends.The 200 lances in the woods, unemployed in their flank-guard role to now, emerged from their hide and plunged into the unguarded rear of Somerset's flank attack. The biter was bit.

Squeezed between the lethal charge of Edward's lancers and Gloucester's stubborn line, and with no help from their centre, still standing as interested lookers-on, Somerset's division broke in confusion and ran from the field. Edmund Beaufort, maddened by the failure of his plans, galloped back to his centre where Wenlock sat, unmoving still and helmetless, and split his skull with one blow of an already bloody battleaxe. Edward, sensing as always the critical moment of battle, urged his own men forward to join again with Richard closing with the now-confused centre of Lancaster's last army and driving them from the stricken field. Hastings, moving forward alongside on the right dealt equally quickly with the Earl of Devon's division and the Battle of Tewkesbury was fought and won and lost, and with it the last hopes of the House of Plantagenet of Lancaster.

Edward Prince of Wales, last sprig of the usurping line sprung from John of Gaunt, lay dead on the Bloody Meadow. Edmund Beaufort, taken in flight, joined him via the headsman's block the following day and the former King, poor, witless Henry VI, long a prisoner in the Tower, died hours later under the knives of his jailers. The board was swept clean and Edward's fighting was done.

Twelve years later, on April 9th 1483 in his Palace of Westminster, with the priests' prayers for his salvation sounding ever more faintly in his ears and the light failing, Edward, fourth ruler of that name and mightiest Warrior-King of the English, slipped down and down into the dark. And was gone.

Ancient Arms of England,
changed by Edward III to incorporate the fleurs-de-lis
to demonstrate his claim to the French crown
as only son of the last surviving child of
Philip IV, "le Bel".

CHAPTER TWO

"... if he were dead, what would betide on me..."

The Queen, Elizabeth Woodville, widow of a poor Lancastrian knight, Sir John Grey, whose body had gone into the grave pits at Towton more than twenty years earlier, leaving her with two young sons, was not present at her husband's passing. A King's deathbed was no place for women, nor in view of her and her family's unpopularity with the Lords and Commons, would she have found a ready welcome had she attended it. In any event Elizabeth had other problems to occupy her, in particular how she and her close kin were to maintain their hold on power in England with their main prop dead.

Elizabeth Woodville was no more popular in the land than her immediate predecessor Margaret of Anjou had been, and for very similar reasons. Both were extravagant, vain and grasping, both continually coaxed and cajoled their husbands for ever more power and wealth to be handed on to their own close (and closed) circle, and both, in the eyes of all but their closest supporters, were jumped-up nobodies, doubly fortunate to attract the favourable notice of a reigning King of England.

Edward had married Elizabeth secretly on May 1st 1464, while en route to the Northeast to deal with yet another uprising in support of Lancaster. He arrived in Newcastle to find that John Neville had already dealt with the problem very efficiently and expeditiously at the Battle of Hexham, and that the arch-traitor, Henry Beaufort third Duke of Somerset who had led the revolt, had been beheaded in accordance with Edward's standing orders. As a mark of his pleasure, the King made Neville Earl of Northumberland and gave him all the lands and castles which went with the title, and which had been held for centuries past by the Percy family. At the same time, Edward maintained his plan to build a counter-weight to the ever-growing power of the Neville family, which was most clearly seen in the authority of its head, the Earl of Warwick, the King's early mentor who in a later age would be titled "Kingmaker".

The Woodvilles were not an obvious choice to balance the Nevilles' all-pervading influence. Their single attribute was that all their women were beauties and their men were handsome; their greatest problem was that they had no standing among the noble houses of the kingdom. Elizabeth set out to rectify matters through the acquisition of titles and lands by marrying her many siblings - the family was notably fruitful - to the holders or heirs of some of the greatest names in the land. In short space her brother John was married to the Dowager Duchess of Norfolk, 50 years his senior, sisters were married to the heirs of the Earls of Essex and Kent and - most disastrously in the longer term - to the youthful Duke of Buckingham, while her father was created Earl Rivers and given the post of Lord Treasurer. Her two sons from her first marriage were ennobled at a later stage, Thomas, the elder, being created Marquess of Dorset, a title rendered vacant in the aftermath of the Battle of Tewkesbury, with his brother created a Baron as Lord Richard Grey.

And now, all was threatened by the death of the family's one, sure shield and they had few illusions as to what would befall them once the King's protection was gone. They retained one last trump card: possession of the new King, Edward, a boy of 13 who at the time of his father's death had his own Court and Council at Ludlow, the old Yorkist fief in the Welsh Borders, where the Queen's brother, Earl Rivers since his father's execution by the Kingmaker, acted as his immediate guardian. If the boy-King could be brought swiftly to London and formally crowned, the Office of Lord Protector of the Kingdom, which Edward had indicated should be filled by his brother Richard, would become redundant and Edward V, under the guidance of his Woodville family, could be manipulated even more successfully than his father before him.

This was the basic strategy decided by the Queen, her sons and her younger brother Sir Edward Woodville, in feverish, drawn-out meetings as the King's end approached and immediately Edward died, Elizabeth despatched couriers to Ludlow, advising Rivers of the King's death and urging him in the strongest terms to lose no time in bringing her son to join her at the Palace of Westminster. For his part, her son Dorset would cultivate still more urgently the contacts he was developing in the royal Council, which, pending the new Protector's arrival in the capital, effectively ruled the kingdom, and thus ensure support for the necessarily speedy arrangements for young Edward's coronation. Meantime, the Queen, her sons and brother could usefully occupy themselves in overseeing the proper disposition of the dead King's personal treasury, held in the Tower of which the Marquis of Dorset was, fortuitously, Constable.

As Edward lay dying in London, his brother Richard, Duke of Gloucester, was at his customary seat at Middleham Castle in the north Yorkshire dales. He preferred the freer, cleaner life of the country to the ceremony and inaction of the royal court and here in Wensleydale he was admirably placed to act as the King's effective Vice-regent in northern England, to keep a weather eye on the shifty Percies in their Alnwick stronghold and to deal with the Scottish raiding incursions which occurred at regular intervals.

Richard and Edward had met for talks two months earlier and while the King's health had not been of the best, there was no indication then of serious illness developing. He was, therefore, surprised and shocked by the news brought to him, not by a messenger from the Council, nor from the Queen, but sent by his old comrade-in-arms from Barnet and Tewkesbury, Lord William Hastings. The message was terse and to the point, the King was dead, he had entrusted Richard with the protection of the kingdom and his heir, and Gloucester must get to London quickly to ensure that Edward's wishes were carried out and in the interest of his own safety.

Puzzled by the apparent urgency of Hastings' plea, Richard commenced preparations to move to London, meantime writing to Earl Rivers at Ludlow to ask where best he could meet with his nephew's train to ensure that they arrived together in London. There was no speedy response from Rivers, instead two other messengers arrived, one from Hastings again urging the utmost haste on Gloucester and advising him that the Woodvilles had taken over the Council and bid fair to do likewise for the Kingdom. The second courier came from Henry Stafford, the young Duke of Buckingham, married, perforce, to Katherine Woodville years before and now eager to ally himself with Richard to ensure that sufficient power would be available to deal properly with his despised in-laws.

Realising at last what problems were in the wind, Richard hastened his preparations and sent to Buckingham that he would meet with him on the road south to London. Further, he wrote to Queen Elizabeth, commiserating with her on their joint loss and promising loyalty to the new King. He added that it would be inappropriate for the Council to make any major enactments before the King and he reached the capital, since these would, in fact, be unlawful. He then set out for York where, before turning south on the London road, he arranged for all the local dignitaries to swear fealty to the new King, Edward V.

Nearing Nottingham, Richard met a courier from Earl Rivers with news that the young King's train expected to reach Northampton by the end of April and they would look forward to meeting him there and journeying on to London together. Since the proposed arrangement gave ample time for the two parties to rendezvous, Richard slowed his march, reaching Nottingham on the 26th of the month. Here he received further messages from Buckingham, to whom he replied suggesting a rendezvous with his party at Northampton, and from Hastings, in which his old comrade advised of the developing Woodville coup through their dominance of the Council and their (now) clear intention to rule England through a boy-King, whose coronation had been provisionally set for May 4th.

Richard of Gloucester reached Northampton, scene of his brother Edward's first victory over Lancaster 23 years earlier, on April 29th to find that the royal train had arrived the day before and had moved on to Stony Stratford, fourteen miles south along the London road. Couriers from Buckingham were waiting his arrival at Northampton with news that the Duke expected to join him there that night. Gloucester decided his best course was to await Buckingham's arrival and then to press on with all possible haste after the King's party.

Buckingham arrived in time to join Richard for the evening meal and, probably to their surprise, a further guest arrived, Earl Rivers, who explained that he had taken the royal train further down the road to the capital as he did not think there would be quarters in Northampton sufficient to billet both parties. The three spent an enjoyable evening together before Rivers left to seek lodging, leaving the two Dukes together to continue their talk.

Richard knew little of Henry Stafford, second Duke of Buckingham, nor for that matter did the country at large. The first Duke, Buckingham's grandfather, was directly descended from Thomas of Woodstock, youngest son of Edward III and had died at Northampton fighting for Lancaster; his father the Earl of Stafford had been killed five years before that at First St Albans, fighting in Lancaster's cause alongside his father-in-law, Edmund Beaufort, Duke of Somerset. Thus Buckingham, at 30 of an age with Richard, had blood royal aplenty in his veins and aged only 12 had become the owner of broad estates and castles in south Wales and along the Marches. On all counts, therefore, he was an obvious target for the aggrandisement of the Woodville family and Queen Elizabeth had seen to it that he married her sister Katherine, who was some years his senior, well before he reached adulthood.

Henry Stafford.
Second Duke of Buckingham

(Engraving taken from a traditional portrait)

The enforced relationship with the Woodvilles was not to Buckingham's liking - to say the least. As a direct descendant of Edward III through both parents, he resented the contrived alliance with a family of commoners and his resentment grew to hatred with the passage of time. Once he was old enough to manage his own affairs, he took himself off to his favourite castle at Brecknock and played little or no part in affairs of state before or after Edward IV's final triumph over Lancaster in 1471, but he continued to nurse his grievance against the Queen and her family until it became obsessional. And now at last, with King Edward's death, he sensed his time had come. The Woodvilles' great protector was no more and power must revert to those whose birth fitted them to rule, of whom the two greatest examplars were undoubtedly himself and Richard of Gloucester.

What passed between the two Plantagenets that evening in Northampton was not recorded by either, but the outcome of their discussion quickly became plain with the morning. The lodgings taken by Earl Rivers were surrounded before dawn broke, his escort was disarmed and the Earl himself was taken into custody. Gloucester and Buckingham then rode on to Stony Stratford, where the new King's party had already assembled to move further towards London. Here they took the young King into protective custody, arrested the leaders of his escort, Lord Richard Grey his half-brother, and Sir Thomas Vaughan his Chamberlain (a faithful supporter of the Woodvilles) and dispersed the 2,000 men who had accompanied the King from Ludlow back to their homes. The Dukes then returned to Northampton with the King, and Richard sent couriers to Hastings in London to advise him of the coup and to seek his further advice in light of developments after news of the Woodvilles' discomfiture arrived.

In London, the Queen and Dorset were roused from their beds by messengers bearing news of Richard's decisive move and realised that, without possession of the King, the game was over. Sir Edward Woodville had left with the fleet - and his share of Edward's treasure - that very morning to prevent Lord Hastings summoning reinforcements from Calais, and frantic calls for help to erstwhile supporters in the Council were either ignored or drew a hostile response. Clearly the Woodville faction, with their greatest supporter dead, many of their chief players absent or imprisoned, and lacking their remaining trump card, carried little real weight in the realm's councils and could look for scant mercy at Gloucester's hands once he learned how they had planned to take over the rule of the kingdom. The only hope was to take the same course used twice previously by the Queen at times when the Yorkist cause had faltered and, with her other children, flee to the sanctuary of Westminster Abbey. Thoughtfully, the Marquis arranged to have the balance of King Edward's treasury transferred from the Tower to the Abbey at the same time. It would be safer for all concerned, he felt, to have it under his immediate control.

The despair of the Woodvilles was nicely balanced by the euphoria of the older nobility, led by the late King's oldest friend and confidant, William Hastings, the Lord Chamberlain. He had heard from Richard of his successful counter-move to take possession of the King's person and of the arrest of Earl Rivers, Richard Grey and Vaughan, who had been sent to Yorkshire under strong escort to await their respective fates. Meantime, the Lord Protector, with his faithful ally Buckingham, would bring the King to London and expect to reach the capital by Sunday, May 4th. Hastings wasted no time in sending his congratulations and busied himself with preparations for the royal arrival. Once these formalities were completed, he would confer at length with Gloucester on the best way of dealing with the Queen Dowager and the Marquis of Dorset. Ways must be found to draw their venom permanently.

Between Woodvilles' despair and Hastings' delight, the Chancellor of England, Thomas Rotherham, Archbishop of York, ran hither and thither. His first inclination was to support the Queen and her house and, in token of his esteem for her and her cause, he gave the Great Seal into her keeping at the Abbey. Then, considering which side was likely to wield the more immediate power in London, he sent for the return of the Seal, which should, perhaps, be more properly kept in his own hands, pending the arrival of the King and the Protector. Two other key players, the while, kept their heads better than the Archbishop and waited on the wheel's next turning.

First was Thomas, Lord Stanley, leading member of the Privy Council, lean, bearded and greying, one of the great survivors of the Roses conflict and comrade-in-arms of the new Protector at whose side he had fought in the last Scottish campaign. Stanley was the greatest magnate in the Northwest since the fall of the Nevilles and fourth husband to Margaret Beaufort, direct descendant of John of Gaunt, independently wealthy, and with an only child, Henry Tudor, self-styled Earl of Richmond, who had spent most of his life exiled in France.

The second was a man of the cloth, who, following conversion to the Yorkist cause after Tewkesbury, had risen high in the councils of his new master, Edward IV. He was short, rotund, cherubic even, and at 63 years of age vastly experienced in the governance of the realm and the shrewdest man in the Kingdom, one John Morton, formerly Master of the Rolls, now Bishop of Ely, Member of the royal Council, and beneath his benign manner an unrepentant supporter of Lancaster who sensed that the times were a-changing. The main prop of York was gone, the Woodvilles and their presumptious ambitions thrown into the discard. With the World turned upside down, what mischief might not be possible to one who had spent much of his life as a power behind the throne, planning, plotting, manipulating ? The amiable, gentle-spoken man of God awaited coming events with an assurance developed over decades of learning, tempered in the furnace of war and matured through constant swings of chance between disaster and success. His hour was nearly come.

Detail from contemporary sketch of
the Badge of William, Lord Hastings,
believed to incorporate Hastings' face.

CHAPTER THREE

"... his common designation was 'The Parson of Blokesworth' ..."

John Morton was born in 1420 near the hamlet of Milborne Styleham in Dorset. Eldest of five sons of a small landowner, his early education was at the nearby Cerne Abbey, where his uncle was Prior and where the Benedictines taught him Classics and, much more importantly, the organisation and administration of business affairs, skills which were notably lacking in the wide world outside. He went on to Balliol College at Oxford, becoming a vice-chancellor at 26 and took deacon's and priest's orders at 28. By the time he was 31, he had qualified as LL.D in Civil and Canon Law and was collecting profitable clerical appointments, becoming Prebendary of Corringham in Lincolnshire and then Parson of Blokesworth, near his birthplace and some eight miles from Blandford.

He divided his time between Oxford, Blokesworth and London where there was good business to be done in the Law Courts and Morton was soon acknowledged as one of the leading legal practitioners, gaining the notice of Thomas Bourchier, Archbishop of Canterbury, who recommended him to Henry VI. This led to his appointment as a clerk to the Privy Council and, additional to Blokesworth, he was given the Prebend of Fordington in Salisbury diocese. Thus as the war clouds gathered over the Kingdom, John Morton stood high in the councils and favour of the House of Lancaster and when the bloody field of Towton was fought, he was in York with Henry and his Queen, Margaret of Anjou, doubtless offering fervent, if fruitless, prayers for the success of the Red Rose.

When news of the catastrophe for Lancaster reached the city in the last hours of Palm Sunday 1461, all was panic-struck confusion and, taking what possessions they could easily carry with them, the royal party, Morton among them, fled northwards to the safety of the Scottish Borders and thence to Edinburgh to beg and bargain for assistance from Scotland's King. Eighteen months later, separated from the King, Morton was with the Queen's party in France where they were effectively exiled during the first eight years of Edward IV's reign, until Warwick and his new son-in-law, George, Duke of

Clarence, next brother to the King and the Kingmaker's selected candidate to take over the crown, were themselves forced to flee to the French court to escape Edward's vengeance.

Louis, the Spider King of France, and Morton, arch manipulators both, saw clearly the threat to Yorkist dominion which would emerge from an alliance of the two bitter enemies, Margaret and Warwick, and worked subtly and separately towards a reconciliation. Theirs was no easy task, but by August, 1470, Queen and Earl were brought together at Angers and formally reconciled, Warwick's younger daughter, Anne Neville being married to Margaret's son, Edward, Prince of Wales as a token of the new alliance. Then, with money and men supplied by Louis, and accompanied in his train by Morton with a 'watching brief' for the Queen, Warwick returned to England and aided by his brother John, Marquis Montagu, set Henry VI back on the throne, while Edward in a reversal of roles fled to exile in Burgundy. Margaret stayed in France until Warwick could guarantee her security in England and did not arrive until Easter Day of 1471, which ironically was the day of Warwick's defeat and death at the Battle of Barnet.

Morton had travelled south in Warwick's train from Coventry to Barnet, expecting to witness the Earl's final victory over the Yorkist usurper. When all his hopes were shattered in the defeat and death of the Kingmaker, he took to horse again, making his way this time westwards to the continuing hope offered by the Queen's return and the growing strength of Somerset and Jasper Tudor in her cause. In the final disaster at Tewkesbury, ending once for all Lancaster's dream of retaking the Kingdom, Morton saw no other option than to come in from the cold and he made his peace with King Edward, who welcomed the services of so able a servant and made him Master of the Rolls in which post he worked hard and skillfully to bring the royal Council's records into something like the regularity and form which would have won the approval of his early Benedictine mentors.

By 1474, Edward was gathering funds and men to reassert the Plantagenet claim to the throne of France and was ably assisted in the first by Morton, who was to show in his later service to Henry VII a similar talent for squeezing money from fat, and not so fat, English purses, for the use of his royal master. In July 1475, Edward landed at Calais with a force of 1,500 men at arms and 15,000 archers and was met by ambassadors from Louis, who wanted nothing but peace, and was prepared to pay for it. Edward was agreeable and teams of commissioners from the two sides met to work out terms.

Included in the English team was John Morton, and they were successful in negotiating a nine-year annual payment to Edward of 50,000 crowns and the bethrothal of his daughter, Elizabeth, to the French Dauphin. In addition to various other down-payments to recompense Edward for expenses incurred in his expedition, Louis also agreed to ransom Margaret of Anjou from her four-year imprisonment after Tewkesbury, thus enabling Morton to satisfy any moral debt he may have felt for old favours from the House of Lancaster. At the same time, he was able to feather his own nest by claiming, with Thomas Rotherham, the lion's share of the largesse of 16,000 crowns which Louis sent to the English negotiators.

Returned home, his stock with the King higher than ever, Morton cultivated a closer relationship with the Queen and her Woodville family, who came to rely on his ever-available advice and counsel. Their support was no doubt influential in persuading Edward that Morton was meant for higher things than Mastership of the Rolls and, following the death of the Bishop of Ely in August, 1478, the King nominated Morton to the vacant See, giving him a seat in the Lords and a full place in the Council. Oversight of the Rolls was, conveniently, handed on to Morton's nephew Robert.

John Morton, Bishop of Ely, had finally arrived. Still hale and hearty at nearly 60, he had wealth, position and lands, he had the friendly ear of the King, the Queen and her family, and was appointed to instruct the young Prince of Wales in the virtues becoming to a future king. Yet deep within him burned a flame which was kindled at First St Albans, fanned at Towton and Barnet and Tewkesbury, and which could only be satisfied by the final destruction of the House of Plantagenet of York.

Coat of Arms of John Morton,
Bishop of Ely.

CHAPTER FOUR

" ... Stanley, look to your wife; if she convey
Letters to Richmond, you shall answer it... "

homas, second Lord Stanley, was the great Trimmer of the latter
years of the Plantagenet dynasty. A powerful magnate with wide
lands in North Wales and the Northwest of England, his support was
valued by successive monarchs of both factions within the ruling House and
his allegiance moved easily between Red and White Rose as circumstances
required. A well-educated man with literary pretensions, he had the knack of
making himself useful to the King-of-the-moment and had risen high in the
Council of Edward IV, taking his place in the "inner Cabinet of Greybeards"
with Lord Hastings, Thomas Rotherham the Archbishop of York and John
Morton.

Stanley was the fourth husband of Margaret Beaufort, Countess of
Richmond, only child of John, first Duke of Somerset, and sole survivor of
the senior branch of the bastard royal line descended from the doubly
adulterous relationship between John of Gaunt, third surviving son of Edward
III, and Katherine Swynford. Slightly built, tight-lipped, eyes hooded,
independently wealthy through her descent from the Holland family, Earls of
Kent, Margaret survived the years of Yorkist dominance with her person and
fortune intact due largely to her choice of spouse. Her first marriage, in
infancy, to John de la Pole, son of the first Duke of Suffolk was dissolved after
three years and, as one of the richest heiresses in the realm, she was thought
a suitable bride for the half-brother of Henry VI, on whose wish she married
Edmund Tudor, Earl of Richmond, in 1455. Although his bride was only 12
years of age, Tudor lost little time in cementing his fortunate alliance and
Margaret's first and only child, Henry, was born at Pembroke Castle on
January 28th, 1457. Richmond never saw his son, having died of plague some
months before the birth, following a period of imprisonment after First St
Albans.

In short space, Margaret, still short of her fourteenth birthday, travelled
with her brother-in-law, Jasper Tudor, to Greenfield Manor near Newport,

Miniature of Margaret Beaufort by Lucas Hornebulte

Collection V de S

where her third marriage, to Henry Stafford, second son of another staunch Lancastrian, Humphrey, Duke of Buckingham, was arranged and celebrated at Lichfield on January 3rd, 1458. Within a space of just over three years, Margaret Beaufort's new father-in-law died fighting for Lancaster at Northampton in July 1460 and her husband was with the army of the Red Rose beaten at Towton on Palm Sunday, 1461, but made his submission to Edward immediately afterwards and thereafter maintained loyalty to the Yorkist cause, suffering serious hurt at Barnet ten years later, fighting for Edward against the Kingmaker's army. His wounds proved mortal and he died in the early October of 1471.

The Battle of Tewkesbury and its aftermath had left Margaret Beaufort as the highest-born survivor of the Lancastrian House. Her only son, Henry Tudor, had found refuge in Brittany, where he had fled with his uncle, Jasper Tudor, to escape the retribution Edward IV was visiting on the few remnants of Lancaster. Her own loyalty was not in immediate doubt, it could hardly be otherwise with her husband mortally hurt fighting for the King, but with Stafford's death, she realised her vital need for a speedy, new alliance to ensure the future security of herself and her many possessions. Lord Thomas Stanley, widower (his late wife, Eleanor Neville was sister to the Kingmaker) owner of broad estates in Cheshire and North Wales, Steward to King Edward's household, suited her requirements perfectly and they were married at the beginning of June 1472, an interval of widowhood much less than the minimum twelve months thought "proper".

Post-nuptial arrangements were dealt with in most business-like fashion to the satisfaction of both parties, with Stanley taking a life interest in his wife's considerable holdings of land in south England and the Midlands, and she having a yearly income of 500 marks from his estates. As further insurance against any doubts of her loyalty which might rise in the King's mind, the new Lady Stanley took care to develop her husband's linkage with the Woodvilles, to whom he was already related through his son's marriage. By 1480, her friendship with Edward's Queen had become sufficiently close for Margaret to bear the latest royal Princess, Bridget, to her christening at the new royal palace at Eltham - a mark of signal favour.

Only three years later, with Edward dead, the Woodvilles scattered, and a new Protector moving steadily and decisively towards London to take on the re-ordering of the Kingdom, Margaret Beaufort knew that she must, yet again, re-order her own affairs, First to assure survival, then - perhaps - to take advantage of such opportunities as might appear from this new melting-pot to the benefit of her still-exiled son, Henry Tudor. She must take counsel with her husband, and with that shrewd, subtle and sympathetic man John Morton, Bishop of Ely, to determine the best course for Beaufort and Stanley, for Tudor and Lancaster, and - of course - for England.

Arms and signature of Margaret Beaufort.
The Bordelure indicates the family's legitimation.

CHAPTER FIVE

"...Welcome, sweet Prince, to London, to your chamber..."

Richard of Gloucester, Lord Protector of England, arrived at the gates of London with his ward, Edward V, and his new comrade-in-arms, Henry Stafford, Duke of Buckingham, in the morning of Sunday, May 4th 1483. They were accompanied by 500 gentlemen from Wales and north England, riding without armour, and were joined by an equal number of notables from the city for the new King's first entry into his capital. The procession moved through cheering crowds to the cathedral of St Paul's and on to the Palace of the Bishop of London, where the King would lodge for the time being.

The essential pageantry completed, Gloucester moved quickly to re-establish stability in the country's government and, at his first Council meeting, was formally accepted as Protector and Defender of the Realm, and given powers of Regency, pending the Coronation of Edward V. That formality out of the way, Richard rearranged the main Offices of the Crown in accordance with his own wishes and in light of developments after King Edward's death. The Great Seal was taken from the unstable grasp of the Archbishop of York and his Office as Chancellor given to the Bishop of Lincoln, John Russell, a skilled and experienced diplomat who had served Edward IV faithfully and well. Russell's former post as Keeper of the Seal went to John Gunthorpe, Dean of Wells, another man of great learning and a long-time Counsellor to the late King. William Hastings was confirmed in his posts as Lord Chamberlain and Captain of Calais, as were the existing judges and officials of the Treasury, the only exception being the installation of John Wood, a former Speaker of the Commons and friend of the Protector, as Treasurer. Lord Stanley continued his Stewardship of the royal Household, and Henry Stafford, Duke of Buckingham was made a member of the Council.

In a series of following meetings, a new date, June 24th, was set for the Coronation of Edward V, the King's lodging was moved to the Tower, still the greatest fortress in the land, the continued imprisonment of the Woodvilles and Vaughan was agreed, and Sir Edward Woodville and the Marquess of

Dorset were outlawed and a price put on their heads. Envoys were sent to Woodville's fleet, then lying in the Downs, to publish his outlawry and offer pardon to all men who would desert him, a tactic which succeeded so well that Woodville, finding himself with only a single remaining consort to his own vessel, set course for Brittany, still guarding his own share of the late King's treasure.

All of the initial decisions and provisions of the Protector in Council sat well with the two former pillars of Edward IV's power, Lords Hastings and Stanley. With the Woodvilles' party broken, theirs was the only surviving grouping from the old regime and Hastings, ever the ebullient, hail-fellow-well-met leader of the late King's strongest faction at court, was pleased to add the allegiance of two formerly distinguished props of the Woodvilles, Thomas Rotherham, Archbishop of York, and John Morton, Bishop of Ely to his own party. Rotherham might be a dithering fool, but he was still the second Churchman of England, while Morton was accounted by his former master, Edward, the best brain in the Kingdom, and came strongly recommended by Lord Stanley as an undoubted asset to their position as the real power behind the new Protector. Morton, and for that matter Stanley himself, had been strong supporters of Lancaster in days gone by of course, but - pish - those days had ended 12 years before on the sunlit meadows of Tewkesbury. They were all Yorkists now.

The only shadow on Hastings' enjoyment of the fruits of his fidelity to the cause of the House of York - which included the enjoyment of his late King's mistress, Jane Shore - was the obvious intimacy which had sprung up between the Lord Protector and Henry Stafford. Although a new member of Council (King Edward had never considered him fitted for such a role despite his royal lineage) Buckingham was regularly the first to proffer advice at meetings and Richard seemed always to lean towards the new man's way of thinking. Admittedly, Buckingham had been the first to join with Richard after the King died and had helped with the arrest of the Woodvilles and the dispersal of the force which accompanied the new King from Wales. But where was Buckingham at Barnet and Tewkesbury ? And where, for that matter, was Gloucester at Towton and Mortimer's Cross?

A dwindling few had grown grey and scarred in the service of York, and their sage advice should not now be disregarded in favour of the thinking of new-made men like Buckingham - and the boys Gloucester had brought with him from the north, Lovell and the others. This, at least, was the thinking of John Morton – and Stanley and Hastings found much in it to agree with. He would have to keep a careful eye on developments to ensure that his pre-eminence in the governance of the Realm was in no way diminished, either before or after the coronation of the new King, son of his dear friend and old master.

❖   ❖   ❖

The inner core of the Council's Old Guard met regularly at the almost-daily gatherings of the land's ruling body called by the Protector, but found it progressively expedient to meet in the evenings at each other's houses. Here, ostensibly, they dined together in good fellowship, old friends enjoying each other's company after another day's labour for the benefit of the realm.

More and more, however, as the days of May slipped by and the King's coronation drew nearer, the talk revolved around the Protector's preference for advice from the northern incomers and above all from his friend of a few short weeks, the Duke of Buckingham. Already, Buckingham had been appointed Constable of royal castles in the west and southwest with powers to summon the armed arrays within those counties. He was made Steward of the king's lands there, an office of great potential profit, and as the flow of grants and dignities continued, Henry Stafford became ever more obnoxious to the gnarled old warrior, Hastings. Where was all this leading and, more important, what would William Hastings' standing in the Land be worth if the present state of affairs continued ?

Stanley drew bitter comparisons between Buckingham's aggrandisement and the lack of favours for more-experienced and worthier peers like Hastings and, come to that, himself. Where would Richard have been without Hastings' timely advice on the manoeuvring which developed after Edward's death and who but they had stood firm in Council against the plotting of the Woodville faction ? That worldly man of God, John Morton, old Lancastrian and former friend of the Woodvilles, could clearly take an even-handed view of the growing differences between Lord Hastings and the Buckingham faction surrounding the Protector and, with his years of experience in the Law Courts and administration of the rule of the country, was able (on Stanley's urging) to provide clear and cogent analysis of the developing situation, and promised that trusted agents would continue to monitor the activities of the other faction and thus enable Hastings' party to plan any necessary corrrective action at the appropriate time.

For the moment, Morton recommended nothing be done which could alert the others to the detailed scrutiny under which their plans and schemes were coming, though it would probably be prudent to take precautions against surprise moves, for example by ensuring the immediate availability of loyal men-at-arms in sufficient numbers to prevent any possibility of a coup d' etat. Hastings, the old destrier-turned-courtier, found it difficult to follow some of Morton's more convoluted reasoning but he was clearly a man of great intelligence who had stood high in the regard of King Edward, and seemed to have good sources of information within the enemy camp. Moreover, Stanley believed the Bishop's information to be accurate and was clearly convinced by his interpretation of the facts.

After his guests had taken their leave, Hastings mused over their talk and decided the advice was sound. He would play the waiting game, as Morton suggested and, moving to happier thoughts, Jane Shore was waiting his pleasure in his private chamber. Life was full and good; he had loyal friends, wealth and power, and a charming mistresss and the upstart Buckingham would soon rue the day he tried to supplant the last of Edward's Praetorians.

While William Hastings prepared for his tryst with Jane Shore, Lord Stanley and the Bishop of Ely had less romantic business to transact. At Stanley's house, Margaret Beaufort had been sharing an evening meal with her nephew the Duke of Buckingham and now awaited the return of her husband who, with John Morton, she promised would have startling revelations concerning plots they feared were afoot against the well-being of the State. Clearly, these were matters of which Buckingham, as the Protector's closest and most trusted confidant, should be advised and she was sure they could depend on Buckingham's discretion in maintaining the confidentiality of his sources. Likewise, the advice of the vastly experienced Morton would be invaluable on the timing of any necessary counter measures and she was certain the worldly-wise Bishop wished for nothing better than to attach himself to the new rising star of the Protector's inner Council and to serve his interests.

Glowing in this approbation of his ever-rising status in the Kingdom, Henry Stafford awaited impatiently the arrival of his uncle by marriage, Thomas, second Lord Stanley, and his colleague the Bishop of Ely, formerly known, Stafford recalled, as the Parson of Blokesworth. Soon, footsteps sounded in the stone-flagged hall and Stanley entered, Morton following. Greetings exchanged, the four sat to talk. The three Deceivers had joined with their unwitting accomplice and in the shadowy corners of the room where they talked, the ghosts of Lancaster gathered, rustling, whispering, listening...

Arms and signature of William, Lord Hastings.

CHAPTER SIX

"... tell me what they deserve
That do conspire my death with devilish plots ..."

Buckingham's Plantagenet ancestry was all too apparent when Stanley - playing the bluff, plain-spoken northcountryman - revealed their doubts on Hastings' loyalty to the Protector. He raged at Hastings' falseness and was of a mind to rush immediately to Richard with the news of his supposed-friend's treason. Morton, subtle counterpart to Stanley, suggested that premature disclosure would not best serve their purpose; they had no firm evidence yet of the plot the Lord Chamberlain was constructing and Hastings would simply deny any accusation and demand that hard evidence was produced to confirm the charges made against him. Further, there were indications that the Queen and her son, Dorset, could well be involved in the plot and his Grace of Buckingham would appreciate better than most the potential for harm that would stem from any resurgence of the Woodville influence.

All in all, best to leave things to mature for a few days more, a week perhaps, by which time definite proof of Hastings' treachery should be forthcoming and could be taken to my Lord of Gloucester who would assuredly act immediately to crush the vipers' nest. In the interim, it would clearly be best if the plotters' suspicions were not aroused by any obvious linkage between Morton and Stanley on the one hand, and Buckingham on the other. Happily this presented no difficulty, since what could be more natural than that the Duke would wish, from time to time, to see his aunt, the Lady Margaret Beaufort, who was privy to all her husband's thoughts and could advise her nephew of every development as it arose. Again, Lady Margaret, her husband, and Morton were all well connected with the Woodvilles and would have little difficulty in discovering the depth of their involvement in the plotting, of which my Lord of Buckingham would be the first to hear.

Satisfied, Buckingham returned to his own lodgings, happy in the thought that he would shortly be able, yet again, to prove the value of his service to his cousin Gloucester, while simultaneously bringing about the downfall of that old lecher Hastings, who continually tried to overbear Henry

Stafford's shrewd contributions at Council with rumblings about new-men and his own great services to York in battles long past. And, if Woodville connivance could also be proven, that would surely write a final finis to that low-born family's influence in great affairs and complete his own revenge for the Queen's insult in marrying his blood-royal with that of her sister. Memories of that years-old wrong, as always happened, made the blood pound in Buckingham's brain and he had half a mind to go to the Protector and.... But no, Morton was right. Best to wait and make doubly sure. A shrewd fellow the worthy Bishop, enormously experienced, quite likeable - could be a good adviser for a great Statesman. Yes, he would certainly keep that point very much in mind.

In the days that followed, Margaret Beaufort took to sending her personal physician on regular visits to Westminster and, on occasion, herself visited the Queen, Elizabeth Woodville, in her self-imposed sanctuary in the Abbey. With her she took small comforts of dainty foods and wine and news of the Protector's schemes to take the crown from her son and to deal ever-more harshly with the Woodville family and supporters and, eventually, even with the Queen herself. At the same time, she comforted the distraught Elizabeth with reports of possible countermoves planned by members of the Council, who were opposed to Richard of Gloucester and his acolyte, Buckingham. If these loyal men could secure the leadership of that ever-faithful supporter of the late King, the powerful Lord Hastings, then all things might be achieved. It was true, of course, that Hastings and the Woodvilles had sometimes not quite seen eye-to-eye on affairs of state, but the threat to young Edward's throne must wipe away former rivalries and all must work together to ensure the legitimate succession.

Speaking of which, Margaret knew the Queen - strangely, so some had thought - had always had friendly relations with Jane Shore, who was now Hastings' dear friend, and if Her Grace could get word to Jane of the need for Hastings to be persuaded to use his influence against Gloucester, then who knew what could come of it. Elizabeth Woodville agreed instantly, Hastings must be persuaded to aid their cause - different arrangements could always be made after her son was crowned - and what woman knew better the power of pillow-talk to influence a man ? She summoned her most trustworthy equerry.

Lord Stanley and John Morton continued to cultivate the doubts and fears and bitter resentment of Lord Hastings in regular evening meetings. They agreed with him that the poisonous barbs of Buckingham in Council (which seemed to have increased recently) could not be much longer endured and expressed surprise that the Protector - Hastings' old comrade - did not take his side more. Still, once the young Edward was crowned, things would surely change and no doubt Buckingham would be returned to his country-exile in Brecknock, Gloucester would be sent back to Middleham to vent his spleen on the Scots, and all would be well again at the court of King Edward V, who would blossom as his father had done under the shrewd tutelage of William Hastings.

And then, the thunderbolt. Buckingham arrived at Stanley's house in the early evening beside himself with excitement. Robert Stillington, Bishop of Bath and Wells and former Chancellor to Edward IV had told the Protector in private audience that his brother's marriage was invalid and his children bastards. Stillington himself had witnessed the formal betrothal of Edward to Lady Eleanor Butler, daughter of the Earl of Shrewsbury, which had taken place before he had met Elizabeth Woodville. There could be no question now of Edward V, so-called, being allowed to succeed to the throne. All this from Gloucester, in strictest confidence of course, and now he must get back to Richard to see what services he could immediately render to the new, true King, to whom, he was sure, Stanley and Morton would give loyal support. Following Buckingham's hurried departure, Margaret Beaufort, Thomas Stanley and John Morton considered the tidings with a sense of growing anticipation, of excitement - they knew their moment had come.

The next morning, there being no meeting of the Council, Morton and Stanley arrived early at Hastings' house and told him what had transpired. It was clear the Protector intended to seize the crown and that instant counteraction was essential if the young King's rights were not to be ridden over roughshod. In the next hours, it was agreed that men-at-arms loyal to Hastings and suitably disguised would be filtered into the White Tower as soon as notice of the next meeting of Council was called. Immediately Council had assembled, Hastings' troops would occupy the ante-room to the Chamber and, on his signal, would burst in on the meeting and arrest the Protector and Buckingham. If they resisted, they would be killed. To ensure that the essential preparations had been successfully completed, it was arranged that Morton should leave the Chamber, ostensibly to send to his house in Holborn for strawberries at Hastings' request, with the signal that all was prepared being his return to the meeting to say that the fruit was on its way.

The same evening, Buckingham met Margaret Beaufort at Stanley's house and was given full details of Hastings' perfidy and of the Queen's and Jane Shore's involvement in its planning. His emotions penduluming between delight and rage, Buckingham flung out of the house and raced to see the Protector and reveal the treasonous conspiracy his agents had uncovered. Richard, at first unwilling to believe Hastings could be involved in such treachery, where his own death could figure as a mere detail, agreed nevertheless that it would be only prudent to put counter measures in train. The guard in the antechamber would be his own men and the introduction of others would be prevented at the entrance to the White Tower. Then he would wait to see if Hastings would condemn himself with his request to the Bishop of Ely.

With Buckingham, he agreed notice of the meeting would be sent out next day and those called would be limited to the men identified as having knowledge of the plan. Immediately, he would send couriers to his loyal friends in the north country asking for reinforcements to be sent urgently, in case the Woodvilles and their remaining sympathisers tried to use the evidence of discord in ruling circles to foment trouble in the streets of the capital. Then, as Buckingham left him to arrange the placing of the guard, Richard summoned his secretary and, with a sad heart, but with the beginnings of Plantagenet rage stirring within him, he started to dictate his letters to the north and the summons to Council, which would take place on Friday the 13th of June 1483 at ten of the clock.

Thirty six hours later, the Council members assembled in their Chamber in the White Tower. Buckingham took his usual seat at Richard's right hand, Hastings, Stanley, and the two clerics Thomas Rotherham and John Morton joined them at the table and as they seated themselves, Hastings asked Morton whether he had strawberries to spare from his garden. The Bishop excused himself saying he would send for a supply, and returned shortly to say that all was arranged. Gloucester called the meeting to order, anger mounting within him, and said he had called Council to consider news which had reached him earlier that week bearing on the King's crowning. However, he must first raise a more immediate problem, namely a new conspiracy against his government and the very lives of himself and his friends. How should he deal with the persons involved in such a plot ?

Clearly, there was but one answer the assembled members could give: those involved should themselves be killed. At which, Richard, in full flush of Plantagenet fury raised his fist and crashed it down on the table. The door was flung open and amid cries of "Treason" stewards and soldiers rushed in and seized Hastings, roughly brushing against Stanley who fell against the table, cutting his head, while, under Buckingham's direction, the other Counsellors were pushed and hustled into the far corner of the room. Lord Hastings, astounded at the reversal of his plans and mortified by the triumphant air of Buckingham protested his innocence of any charge of treachery, but Gloucester would have none of it. Hastings had pronounced his own guilt and his own sentence which would be carried out immediately. Still protesting, Lord William Hastings was dragged from the Chamber down the stone stairs and through the door of the White Tower. Baulks of timber were piled on the ground outside for building repairs and formed a handy, makeshift block on which, after a brief moment for shriving himself, this pillar of York's cause, survivor of battles, bon vivant, and gull, met a sharp, abrupt end to his long and distinguished career.

Above, in the Chamber, the Lord Protector considered the remaining members of Council. He was half-disposed to let them follow Hastings but my Lord of Buckingham had suggested they were not truly involved in this wickedness and he wished to speak with him further about it. However, the Lord Archbishop of York would stay in the Tower's apartments pending a final decision; Lord Stanley should return to his house to have his cuts tended and stay there until he was sent for, and the Protector would feel easier if the Bishop of Ely were to be removed far from London for the time being. The Duke of Buckingham had offered to accommodate him in this and accordingly, John Morton would go to Buckingham's castle at Brecknock and be lodged there until he was summoned.

Alone in the Chamber after the others had left, Richard felt the emptiness which always followed anger and knew that another hard decision already waited his attention. How much easier it would have been had Stillington held his peace, or had Edward been less assiduous in his pursuit of fair ladies. But, assuming Stillington had spoken the truth - and Richard feared he had - there was no choice, and like Hastings he supposed, he must follow his own hard road wherever it might lead, to the very end.

Royal Arms of England as borne by Henry VI,
Edward IV and Richard III.
The signature is Edward's, taken from a letter
in French "Votre bon cousin, Edward R."

Richard III

(Society of Artiquaries of London)

CHAPTER SEVEN

"...For God doth know, and you may partly see,
How far I am from the desire of this..."

ord Stanley returned to his house and told his wife of the morning's
events while she attended to his cut head. Their plan had worked
perfectly - one of the three props holding up the House of York had
been eliminated and Margaret would write to her son, Henry, and tell him the
good news. The exile of Morton to Brecknock was unexpected, but
communicating with him would not be a real problem. Her steward, Reginald
Bray, was completely trustworthy and had often carried letters secretly to her
son in Brittany. He could perform the same function with Morton, while
openly bearing messages to her dear nephew and late husband's namesake,
Henry Stafford.

Immediately, there was pressing need for her to talk to Buckingham to
ensure that the often-unpredictable Duke persuaded the Protector of Stanley's
total loyalty to York, and his earnest desire to continue working with
Gloucester. With Stanley safe in his place in the Kingdom's inner Council and
Morton influencing and guiding the thoughts and actions of Buckingham, the
three would still be well placed to take the next opportunity - whenever and
however it arose - to further the interests of Lancaster, of Beaufort and Stanley
and, one day perhaps, of Tudor. Margaret Beaufort, a spider lurking at the
centre of an ever-widening web of intrigue, despatched an urgent message to
Buckingham asking him to come to see her and then sat down at her desk and
started to write to Brittany.

Buckingham arrived that evening and re-assured his aunt that the
Protector had been made aware of her husband's true part in the affair and had
confirmed Stanley's place in his inner counsels. He had likewise assured
Richard of Morton's blameless role in the plot, instancing his co-operation at
the final meeting when he had not conveyed to Hastings that the supposed
assassins in the antechamber were in fact Gloucester's own men. Richard
accepted this reasoning, though feeling that the sharp-witted Bishop could
have realised Hastings' plans had come to naught when he saw the real guards
still in place and quickly turned his coat accordingly, and he had never really

liked Morton. All in all, he would feel more comfortable if the Bishop were lodged in Brecknock for a time and Buckingham, seeing the opportunity to bring Morton more closely into his own service, did not try overly hard to dissuade his master.

While a messenger rode hard for the Welsh Marches to advise Morton's imminent arrival, the Bishop lodged with Buckingham at his London house. The two spent much time together, not as prisoner and gaoler but more as two gentlemen who had done great things, controlled great events, and had each succeeded in reaching the very heights in their chosen fields. Morton would later be described by his pupil, Thomas More, the "Man for All Seasons" of Henry VIII, as short in stature but upright in bearing, amiable, gentle and earnest in conversation. He liked nothing better than to engage another in wordy debate and to win them over to his way of thinking, the which he invariably did since in "the wisdom" - the practical knowledge of mankind - he had no equal. In a later age, he would have been an expert interrogator, a shrewd philosopher, a brain-washer. For now, he was Bishop of Ely, formerly Parson of Blokesworth, loyal Lancastrian, and chatting ever-more amiably with the second most powerful man in the Kingdom, noting his ideas and thought-patterns, his way of reasoning and apparent capriciousness, and drawing out his long-standing hatred of the Woodville family. Fruitful ground indeed for one as accomplished in "the wisdom" as John Morton.

After two or three nights of increasingly companionable discussion, Morton, with a friendly escort and a lengthy baggage train of pack-horses set out for Brecknock. Buckingham remained in London to assist in the great events which were in train at Westminster, but promised that he would join the good Bishop ere long to continue their most enjoyable discourse, and that he expected they would have much to talk over.

On June 25th, twelve days after Hastings' execution, the Parliament of England, Lords and Commons together, assembled at Westminster. Originally summoned to greet their new, young King, Edward V, they learned instead of his disqualification from the succession on grounds of his illegitimacy and on the following day, the whole gathering processed to Baynard's Castle, the London home of Richard's mother Cecily, Duchess of York. Here Buckingham, speaking for the assembly, read their petition to Richard to "take upon you the said crown and Royal Dignity". With some reluctance still apparent in his manner, the Lord Protector said he would accede to the wishes of the three estates and was hailed with great shouts of "Long Live King Richard ", the very acclamation his father had vainly sought 23 years earlier.

The day before, at Pontefract Castle, Earl Rivers, Thomas Vaughan and Lord Richard Grey had been briefly re-united to learn that, because of the involvement of the Queen and others of her family in Hastings' plot against the life of the Protector and their own actions in support of the earlier plot, their lives were forfeit. Given a space to make their peace with God and to write last letters and Testaments, they were executed in the presence of the Earl of Northumberland, Henry Percy, the King's Warden of the Northeast.

The coronation of Richard III took place on Sunday, July 6th, 1483 , amid pomp, circumstance, splendour and general rejoicing. It was the most magnificent royal occasion that any could remember and the Duke of Buckingham clearly relished his central part in the proceedings, having taken on the role traditionally performed by the Duke of Norfolk, England's hereditary Earl Marshal. Lord Stanley was prominent in the procession, bearing the Royal Mace, the badge of the Constable of England - an office which would be conferred on Buckingham during the festivities following the crowning - and Margaret Beaufort bore the Queen's train, another signal mark of honour.

Richard had decided that he would have a second crowning in his favourite city of York and would make a grand tour of his Kingdom en route to his "capital in the North". Before the splendid procession set out on its journey, the King lavished further honours on Buckingham, making him Great Chamberlain - the post formerly held by his rival, Hastings - as well as Constable and, pending the necessary approval of Parliament, giving him 50 manors formerly held by the Stafford family and worth £ 700 per year. It was agreed that, while the King toured his new realm, Buckingham would spend some time in London to keep an eye on any untoward developments there during Richard's absence and would also visit his estates at Brecknock, which had been neglected for some months past. He would expect to join the King's train in the west country to accompany him over at least part of the journey and so, having led the loyal farewells to the Royal party on July 20th, Henry Stafford wasted no time in setting out for Wales, eager to share the tidings of his newly-bestowed distinctions and honours with his new friend and mentor, the Bishop of Ely.

**Roof Boss in Bere Regis Church, said to be of
John Morton who was born in the Parish.**

CHAPTER EIGHT

"...if the world would have gone as I would have wished, king Henry's son had had the crown and not king Edward..."

ohn Morton had settled comfortably at Brecknock. He had books and papers, the freedom of the castle, and the Summer weather here in the Welsh border country was pleasantly warm. News from London had come through Reginald Bray, apparently en route to check on Margaret Beaufort's estates in the west country. Richard's complete acceptance of the reasons for the involvement of the Stanleys in Hastings' plotting was evident in the honoured places allotted to the pair in the coronation celebrations and no further unpleasantness was expected on that score. Similarly, Lady Margaret had resumed her visits to the former Queen, who was constantly in covert touch with Woodville sympathisers scattered through the southern counties of England and with her son, the Marquess of Dorset, who moved secretly around Yorkshire maintaining links there with the few remaining adherents of his family's cause.

Henry Tudor was still in safe haven in Brittany and his mother had raised with him a former notion, dear to her heart, of an alliance between York and Lancaster through marriage with Elizabeth, eldest daughter of the late King. Such a union would solve, finally, the division in the Plantagenet House which had cost England so much blood and treasure these past 30 years and her son had previously shown willingness at least to consider the idea. As Morton knew, the thought had been put to King Edward after Barnet and Tewkesbury had secured his throne, but he had shown little interest in view of his private intention to betroth Elizabeth to the Dauphin. Circumstances had changed drastically since then and Elizabeth Woodville was interested in the idea, but it was unlikely to find much favour with King Richard. Still, it was a desirable objective to keep clearly in mind and she would appreciate the Bishop of Ely's thoughts on it.

Morton destroyed Margaret Beaufort's letter and sat to ponder the idea of a marital alliance between the warring Houses. It was not a new concept and, in theory, it could eliminate the main bone of contention between York and Lancaster by, in effect, combining their claims to the throne through their joint descent from Edward III. In a land which had wearied of war long since and would not welcome the prospect of any revival of strife, a marriage such as Margaret Beaufort envisaged might well attract support strong enough to fan the embers of Lancaster, still smouldering in Wales and the West of England, into flame. It was, therefore, well worthwhile considering, though the new King, for obvious reasons, would not tolerate it for an instant. But, as Lady Stanley had said, circumstances did change - his own life of ups and downs was sufficient evidence of that - and certainly, a new King would be very grateful to any who had played a significant part in his rise to the throne. Yes, he would have to give this possibility serious thought.

There was a further problem, however, which Lady Margaret seemed to have missed. If the reign of King Richard were, somehow, to be terminated and the blood-line of Princess Elizabeth used to legitimise the claims of Henry Tudor, where did that leave her brothers the former, and uncrowned, Edward V and Richard, lately known as the Duke of York ? If Elizabeth's ancestry was sufficiently Royal to confer the crown on Tudor, did not the identical descent of her brothers give them a greater right to the sceptre? And, if Edward - or Richard - were ever to sit on England's throne, would not their first and only loyalty be to their mother's line - a family which he had found agreeable and friendly enough but, at the same time, averse to sharing the fruits of their fortune with others. There was indeed much to ponder over here, but he should pass his initial thoughts on the subject to Margaret Beaufort and see what response they evoked from that noble, far-seeing and - where the interest of her son was concerned - totally ruthless Lady.

He did not wait many days for a reply - Reginald Bray had much to do on the Beaufort estates but could make it in his way to call on the Bishop again shortly on his return journey, if that were convenient. John Morton was agreeable, and noted the dedication of Bray to his mistress's affairs; such loyalty could be very useful to one much involved in confidential matters and he would remember it. After Bray had left, Morton went into the garden, where he could read Margaret Beaufort's letter undisturbed.

The coronation had been a very magnificent occasion and many had noted the honoured roles she and her husband had played in it. Buckingham was full of himself and his high place of trust with the King - he was now Chamberlain and Constable and had been promised the restoration of valuable family estates which Edward had taken following the attainder of the first Duke. Richard had made clear that Buckingham stood second only to himself in all the land and Henry Stafford was basking in his new-found distinction, so different from only three short months ago, when King Edward had found no use for his talents due, no doubt, to the all-pervasive influence of the Woodvilles. At last that family of nobodies had been dealt with appropriately and Buckingham had his rightful place in the sun, always provided of course, that King Richard continued to reign over his new realm.

Buckingham was currently fully occupied with arrangements for the Royal progress to York, but could be expected in Brecknock about the time the King set out on his journey, around July 20th. He was eager to impress Morton (whose good opinion he clearly valued highly) with his achievements and the Lady Margaret wondered, in the King's absence from Westminster, whether there might not be an opportunity to remove further obstacles to the desirable alliance they had discussed.

Tearing the letter into small strips, Morton smiled to himself. A ruthless Lady indeed - and shrewd. Her reasoning had taken exactly the same course as his own and he had no doubt of his ability to implant doubt and fear in Buckingham's mind. And who knew what an unstable Lord High Constable might do, given his long-standing hatred of the Woodvilles, should a subversive threat to his own new magnificence be subtly adduced. When Bray returned, he would give him a verbal reply to Margaret Beaufort: her thoughts were as his own and it might be well if she were away from the Capital for a few weeks, attending, say, to the Stanley estates in the Northwest, or even joining her husband with the King's train as the Royal Progress continued.

Two weeks after the Coronation, Buckingham arrived home and though he had ridden hard and fast from London, he was bouncing with energy and without question a very happy man. The coronation and the following celebrations, he confirmed, had indeed been the most magnificent in living memory and King Richard had thanked him for his prime part in organising the whole affair. As a token of the King's gratitude he was now Lord Great Chamberlain and, as token of the Royal trust in him, he was High Constable of England with power to command England's armies and castles second only to that of Richard himself. His star, nay his comet, was rising fast and ever-higher in the heavens.

John Morton was liberal in his appreciation of the Duke's achievements, though his high place was, of course, no more than the proper due of the senior descendant of Thomas of Woodstock, son of the great Edward III, and he trusted that nothing would happen to affect adversely the upward surge of Buckingham's fortunes. Detecting a note of doubt in Morton's voice, the mercurial Duke's mood immediately swung to suspicion and while the Bishop protested that there was nothing to concern him, Henry Stafford pressed him for an answer with Morton's continual denials making him ever more-eager to discover this unsuspected worm within his golden apple.

At last, Morton - regretting the necessity to spoil his patron's pleasure - revealed that he had had intelligence from one of his sources within the Woodville family of a new plot to dethrone the King and to reinstall the young Edward on the throne. Clearly, it would all come to naught; the Woodvilles were no longer a power, though it was said that Dorset had gathered men and arms in Yorkshire and that the late King's treasure was being applied usefully in France and Brittany to provide mercenary support for the intended coup. And while the King was away from London on his extended tour of the realm there would be a vacuum at the seat of power, which could provide an ideal opportunity for the Queen Elizabeth to re-seat her bastard son in the King's place.

Buckingham considered Morton's news with anger steadily mounting inside him. Would he, would the Kingdom, never be rid of that hateful family? Was he, after all his efforts, his courageous decision to support his cousin Gloucester, his thwarting of Hastings' plot to kill Richard, to be robbed of his just reward ? No. He, Henry Stafford, direct descendant of the mighty Edward III, Duke of Buckingham, Constable and Chamberlain of England, could never - would never - permit that. Thus the Duke raged, flinging about his chamber.

But how best to prevent this wickedness from succeeding ? He turned to the Bishop of Ely, who had advised him so cleverly on the right course to circumvent Hastings' scheming, what would John Morton advise ? Morton agreed the problem was difficult - though he was still unsure of the full danger which might be involved and there was insufficient evidence to interrupt the Royal Progress, perhaps, after all, it might be better to let things lie until Richard returned to Westminster after his crowning in York. Buckingham would have none of this. In the King's absence he was master in London and he could see the situation called for immediate and, if necessary, drastic action to nip this canker in the bud.

In that case, Morton thought, it seemed that the core of the problem lay in the Tower. The bastard Princes were lodged there and without them, the rebellion would have no purpose, no cause. Not an Englishman would draw a sword or longbow for the Woodvilles alone. It followed that, if the Woodville brats could be disposed of in some quiet way, then the whole enterprise would fail, and my Lord of Buckingham was Constable, he could command entry into any fortress in England, including the Tower. The King would never command the deaths of his much-loved brother's sons, but he would surely be grateful to any friend who crushed a plot seriously endangering his newly-gotten crown, and would accept, though with sadness no doubt, that the elimination of the former Princes had been essential to his continued enjoyment of the high Office to which God had called him.

As Morton talked, coldly, calmly, developing his argument with the consummate skill and logic that was his stock-in-trade, Buckingham could see progressively clearly what must be done to safeguard the King and his own high status. The Woodville bastards must be put down quickly and secretly. He would attend to this himself, as he had done with the Hastings' affair, and would then speed after the King to tell him that Henry Stafford had, once more, saved the House of Plantagenet of York from threatening destruction. Surely, Richard's gratitude would know no bounds, as his friend Morton had made clear. Buckingham, with a hurried farewell to the Bishop of Ely, ran from his private chamber, calling for men and horses to be readied immediately. The Constable of England had urgent business in London.

Signature and motto of Henry Stafford, Duke of Buckingham. He signs as "Harre Bokyngham", his motto: Souvente me souvene – "Remember me often".

CHAPTER NINE

"...and is it thus ? Repays he my deep service
With such contempt? Made I him King for this..."

he Duke of Buckingham came up with the royal train at Gloucester
on July 29th and demanded immediate private audience with the
King. Richard dismissed his attendants and took his obviously
overwrought cousin aside into a private chamber, where Buckingham, striding
around the room in his agitation, poured out his story: the reports of a new
plot inspired by the accursed Woodvilles - the old Queen was involved, and
the French and Bretons, and English traitors - the King and all his family, and
Buckingham, were to be slaughtered - and Edward's bastard restored to the
throne. But he, Buckingham had discovered the plot and using his authority
as Constable he had put an end to it. He had removed, permanently, the focus
for this rebellion - or any future plotting. The bastard princes, Edward and
Richard, were no more.

The King was stunned. His nephews - Edward's sons - were dead,
had been foully killed by this hysterical fool because of some trumped-up tale
of rebellion while he was totally involved in his first royal tour of his country,
showing himself to his people, looking forward to his second, symbolic
crowning in York. What was he to do ? He started to the door to summon
guards but stopped in mid-stride. If he arrested Buckingham now and ordered
his summary execution - the man he had raised so high, to whom he had
clearly and publicly given his trust, his friendship - what would be said ?
Would any - could any - believe that he, Richard had not been involved in
some way ? Even that Buckingham was not acting on his orders ?

For now, he could do - nothing. Only turn on his Constable and rage at
him for a purblind fool and a murderer to boot. Buckingham, already high-
strung from the events of the past days, worn from his hard ride to bring his
King the news, responded in kind. Where would Richard have been without
his stalwart support these past months ? Who had thwarted Dorset's scheme
to take over the ruling of the Kingdom ? Who had discovered Hastings'
plotting and thereby saved the King's very life ? And who, now, had removed
the final obstacle to his enjoyment of the throne ? And was this to be all his

thanks? Fool? Murderer ? He had done better to have joined with Hastings, or with his treacherous in-laws than to receive such treatment from the man he had made King.

Richard's rage turned in an instant to cold hatred of the deranged man before him. He saw his error in raising him so high - how could he have been so blind ? What terrible results had stemmed from his mistake. But, Plantagenet subtlety asserted itself. Buckingham's awful crime must wait its just retribution until his own grasp of the Kingdom was secure. Nothing could bring his nephews back to life and, for now, it was imperative to continue his progress through the land to his second crowning in York and ensure that the land stayed at peace, free from alarums. He swallowed his anger and told Buckingham that he should say nothing to anyone of what he had done and return to Brecknock where there must be many matters awaiting his attention. Richard would continue to York and they would talk further on his return to London in the early Autumn.

Buckingham, badly shaken by the unlooked for reception of his wonderful news, exhausted by his own outburst and fearful of the possible consequences of what he had said, agreed. The King and the greatest Peer in the Realm parted; Buckingham called for fresh horses and, within the hour was spurring furiously for Brecknock. He had not liked the look in Richard's eye. The King was dissembling; all he had striven for, his new standing in the realm, was suddenly - and inexplicably - set at risk. He must discuss the King's churlish ingratitude with John Morton without delay and get that shrewd brain working on what might be expected from Richard and how any adverse move might be countered. The Bishop of Ely would know what must be done next.

Back in the safe, friendly haven of Brecknock, Buckingham was able to relax. He ate a late meal with Morton, although his stomach was still churning, and told him of the unexpected reaction from the King to what should have been most welcome news. He could not understand why Richard was not happy, nay delighted, with the speedy initiative he, Buckingham, had taken to stamp out what could have been a dangerous rebellion, nor his mawkish concern for two bastard-boys who were half-Woodville to boot. It was incomprehensible, insane! Be that as it may, he was shrewd enough to see that the formerly friendly relationship with his royal cousin had been shattered beyond repair and he was at something of a loss as to what he should do to ensure his future safety. What would his wise counsellor advise ?

Morton was sympathetic. It was strange indeed that the King should take such an attitude. My Lord of Buckingham had taken swift and effective action to end a perceived threat to his royal master's throne and his thanks was to be treated like a common criminal. Morton had seldom met with such baseness in all his long career in the service of Kings. He had realised, of course, that Richard could never truly replace his brother, Edward; there were weaknesses, evident to a trained eye and mind - which, incidentally, he had never marked in his host, who had as much Plantagenet blood in him as the King - which would always have made him wary of accepting high office under Richard. On the other hand, the King certainly had the Plantagenet temper and the family's ruthless streak in full measure, and the Duke was right to be concerned for his future position in the land - indeed for his very life. Drastic measures were called for and, if Buckingham would give him the night to ponder the matter, he would hope to have good advice for him with the morning.

The next day Buckingham, eagerly, impatiently, summoned Morton to join him in his chamber. Had the Bishop found him an answer ? To the Duke's delight, Morton rather thought that he had. The only sure road to safety must be to replace the King - Buckingham must emulate his distant cousin, the Earl of Warwick, and put a new King on the throne of England. The Duke could himself summon up a great power of loyal, stalwart Welsh and Westcountry men from his estates; the southern counties of England were already a hot-bed of sedition through the efforts of the Woodvilles and, to complete the circle, he felt sure that Buckingham's aunt, Margaret Beaufort, would be eager to seize such a golden opportunity and call on her son, Henry Tudor, to bring a great army from France and Brittany to join in the rebellion. In this way, Richard would easily be toppled, the constant warring between Lancaster and York could be ended for ever by a marriage between Henry and Elizabeth, daughter of Edward IV, and Buckingham would assume the full mantle of Warwick and become the real ruler of England, the true power behind the throne. Thus Buckingham would be saved, his rightful high-place in the Kingdom assured - and his star would stand higher than ever.

The glittering prospect dazzled Buckingham, though he was not too happy about the Woodville involvement; what would they do when they found their chosen King was dead ? The Bishop gently shook his wise, old head. How were they to find out ? The King could not - and Buckingham would not - tell them, and once the rebellion, as it surely must, succeeded, it would matter little what Woodvilles thought. Henry Stafford, Kingmaker, would be in his rightful place as chief sponsor and adviser to a young and inexperienced King. He would be the most powerful man in the land. None would dare to raise a threatening hand or voice against him.

Buckingham could see clearly that the Bishop was right. How wise he had been to mark the wily skills of Morton and harness them to his own ends. He agreed with him that they must send to Margaret Beaufort straight away, asking that Reginald Bray should come to Becknock urgently for consultations. Morton must write immediately, a courier be summoned and despatched to London, there must be no delay in the commencement of this great new enterprise. The Bishop of Ely hastened to his own chamber and sat to write, the while Buckingham day-dreamed of greatness still to come.

Margaret Beaufort read between the lines of Morton's cryptic note, the obstacles in the Tower had been removed and the King had broken with Buckingham in consequence. The Duke, fearing for his very life, had agreed to join in rebellion against Richard and Morton would ensure that he wasted no time in raising men and arms. The Stanleys would know how best to synchronise the planned rising in the west with the schemes of the Woodvilles - who, obviously, should be left in ignorance of events at the Tower - and with an invasion from France led by Henry Tudor. For the first time, as she would confess years later to Polydore Vergil, the Tudor Historian, Margaret Beaufort felt real hope that one day soon, she would see her son raised to his rightful place as the true heir of Lancaster. She would write to him immediately, urging him to press France and Brittany for men and support and to make ready to return when the hour struck.

Meanwhile, after writing to Henry, Bray must leave at once for Brecknock as Morton had asked, first contacting her husband with the King's train to advise him of what had transpired, and she would go to Westminster, to the Abbey, to tell Elizabeth Woodville of this change in all their fortunes and to impress on her that the rising planned by her family and its supporters must be timed to coincide exactly with Buckingham's rebellion in the west.

For the present, she agreed, her husband would remain aloof from the plot, to keep a foot in Richard's camp. In this way they would be constantly aware of the King's plans, and experience had taught them both that Fate had many twists and all wagers should be hedged, especially when the stake was as high as the throne of England. It would be politic and useful, therefore, for Thomas Stanley to keep close with the King, leaving his wife to work with John Morton in furtherance of their scheme to take advantage of this new prospect which a divine Providence had opened before them

Arms of Thomas, second Lord Stanley,
later Earl of Derby

CHAPTER TEN

"...Buckingham back'd with the hardy Welshmen
Is in the field and still his strength increaseth... "

After leaving Gloucester, King Richard continued his slow and stately progress through the Midlands, dealing with State business along the way. He saw envoys from Isabella of Spain at Warwick and wrote to the Spanish Queen proposing a Treaty of Amity between the two Kingdoms; he corresponded with James III of Scotland, who was anxious for an end to the constant Border-fighting, and with Irish Lords, appointing the Earl of Kildare as his Deputy for the next year; and he wrote to Louis, the Spider King of France, confirming that the truce made with his brother, Edward, would stand - at least until its expiry six months later - and sent his letter by the hand of one of his stable grooms, "no more impressive envoy being called for". Richard had plans for France, but these would not concern Louis, who died on August 30th, leaving his young son, Charles VIII, to rule under the Regency of his older sister, Anne.

On the day that Louis passed over to answer for his many sins, Richard with his Queen and his son Edward, newly created Prince of Wales, reached York for his second crowning which formed the climax to a week of pageants, feasting and State occasions. The Royal party stayed in York - the King's favourite city of all his Kingdom - for several more weeks and then separated, Queen Anne and her son making for the old Neville stronghold of Middleham and Richard, conscious that he had been overly long away from London and that the Buckingham problem had still to be dealt with, started south. He did not hasten unduly and effectively continued his Royal Progress through the eastern counties, reaching Lincoln by mid-October. Here he received news brought urgently by hard-riding courier from the capital: the Kentish men were up in revolt and claiming Henry Stafford, Duke of Buckingham as their leader.

With the seat of Government empty and her husband with the King's party, keeping a watchful eye on Richard's movements, Margaret Beaufort had busied herself spinning a new web of intrigue. Reginald Bray was constantly moving between London, the Northwest, Brecknock and the court of Francis of Brittany, carrying messages to and from Morton and Henry Tudor, while she, or her physician, paid regular visits to Queen Elizabeth, still in the sanctuary of Westminster Abbey, to encourage the Woodville faction's scheming to return Edward V to the throne. At the same time, as the most senior survivor of the House of Lancaster, she wrote to the Courtenays, Earls of Devon and other Lancastrian gentry across the southern counties telling them to prepare secretly for revolt. At last came the long-waited news from her son: Francis, Duke of Brittany had promised 5,000 men and ships to carry them, and the fleet would sail for England before the end of October. With her pieces finally in place across the board, Margaret Beaufort, now with her husband on their Cheshire estates, chose the day for the resurrection of Lancaster, the red rose would rise again on October 18th, 1483.

Unhappily for her plans, the men of Kent, impatient as ever for plunder, as they had been when Jack Cade led them to London over 30 years before, were "up" ten days before the appointed date and as John Howard, Duke of Norfolk moved against them to prevent their reaching the Capital, the King was writing to all his Lords, instructing them to rally to his Standard at Leicester by October 22nd. In his summons, Buckingham was named as leader of the rebellion, "false traitor" and "the most untrue creature living", the rift between the King and his greatest ally was made apparent and it was clear that only one of them could survive the coming conflict.

Henry Stafford rode from his castle at Brecknock on October 18th, accompanied by the Bishop of Ely, and led his force of several hundred men east towards the English border. The Duke was nervous - his army was much smaller than he had hoped and he seemed to detect a sullen air on the part of some of the Welsh contingents. Morton laughed away Buckingham's doubts, their company would grow as they marched and the increase in force would encourage all the men; the men of Kent were already at London's gates and the south and southwest were ablaze with rebellion. Richard could not be everywhere at once and Tudor would join with the rebels before October was out, with 5,000 sturdy Bretons at his back. The Yorkist usurper would be cold in his grave long before Christmas and the Duke of Buckingham would be feasting in Westminster Hall having set a new monarch on England's throne. Buckingham warmed to the heady prospect painted by Morton and urged his horse forward, shouting cheery greetings to the men, urging them on to glory. Even the weather - bleak and grey and wet - must improve soon as the new sun of Buckingham rose in the firmament.

But it did not. The army from the Welsh Marches plodded forward through continual rain, soaking the men and their supplies, turning roads into quagmires, flooding fords, chilling them all to the very bone. They came under attack from hit-and-run raids on their flanks and rear by small, well-armed groups faithful to King Richard. Each day their progress grew slower, more painful, and by the time they reached the curiously-named village of Weobley, still miles short of their first target, Hereford, Buckingham's army had started to disintegrate. News came that the King was at Coventry with a great host of well-armed followers marching to deal with his erstwhile ally, and that all who would desert the rebel cause should have full and free pardon. This was the final blow. The army disappeared, washed away in an unrelenting downpour, its members intent only on making their way home as speedily as the roads allowed. Buckingham's rebellion was over without a blow struck.

The Duke, tired from chasing after deserters, hoarse from ordering them - begging them - not to desert his just cause, returned to the Manor House at Weobley to consult with John Morton. His wisdom and experience alone now stood between Buckingham and total disaster. Surely the Bishop would think of some brilliant ploy which might snatch safety from the doom impending. And then, the final blow, John Morton was not there. The Bishop of Ely, that great survivor, had made certain of his escape route before setting out from Brecknock. Well mounted and with only a couple of trusted servants in train Morton was already on his way to the fen-country surrounding his See in Cambridgeshire. Here safe-hiding was assured until he could take boat for Flanders and, from there, make contact again with his fellow-conspirators. It was a pity that the Great Rebellion had come to naught, but it had been a long chance and, at worst, it had removed Richard's last remaining prop. Now the King alone stood between Lancaster and the crown, Morton's duty to his first master and benefactor, long-dead Henry VI, was nearly done.

His army fled, his dreams of greatness collapsed around him and with no subtle adviser to turn to, Buckingham plunged into despair. He stripped off his surcoat and his fine doublet and found dirty, ragged garments discarded in the servants' quarters. These he put on and mounting his mud-spattered horse rode out into the incessant rain to seek refuge. He went north into Shropshire, remembering a former servant, Ralph Bannaster, who worked a small farm near Wem a few miles up the old Roman road. He would find refuge there and perhaps better news would come, perhaps the Kentish men would take London and Henry Tudor join with the rebels in the Southwest to accomplish Richard's final downfall. Buckingham's volatile nature swung once again to hope for better times as he spurred away from the avenging army of the King he believed he had made and had thought he could unmake.

News of the collapse of Buckingham's rebellion reached Richard as he prepared to leave Coventry, so he moved south instead of west and the uneasy alliance of Woodville supporters and old Lancastrians collapsed before him. He reached the town of Salisbury on October 28th and rested his men there. The following day, amid great excitement, a party of heavily armed men led by the Sheriff of Shropshire rode to the King's quarters, in their midst, still clad in servant's cast-off garments and tied to his horse, rode Henry Stafford, Duke of Buckingham. His old servant's fear of the King's vengeance had proved greater than his love for his former master - and there was also the small matter of a reward of £ 1,000 offered for the Duke's capture.

Richard had appointed Sir Ralph Assheton as Vice-Constable of England, pending permanent replacement of the outlawed Buckingham, and he led the Commission which heard Buckingham confess his rebellion against his lawful King and sentenced him to death. Buckingham asked for a personal hearing from the King, but Richard would not speak with him. Apart from his treason, the blood of two young boys - Edward's sons - stained Buckingham's hands and the King had vowed he would never see or speak with him again. The Duke sent again to Richard, saying he had much to tell the King, but without avail. Fortune - again - smiled on John Morton, Thomas Stanley and Margaret Beaufort.

In the morning of Sunday, November 2nd, Henry Stafford, second Duke of Buckingham, erstwhile Constable and Chamberlain of England, direct-descendant of Edward III, prevented by his King's disdain from revealing the identity of the arch-deceivers, was publicly beheaded in Salisbury's market square.

The great rebellion had collapsed. The noble leaders, other than Buckingham, fled to France, the smaller fry were caught and executed. Henry

Tudor on whom so much hope was pinned arrived off the English coast in the first days of November with only two vessels from his fleet of 15, the rest having been scattered by an early Winter storm. Finding no warm greeting on the shore, Tudor turned back to Brittany to wait again the coming of his hour, offering meanwhile, filial prayers that his mother's key role in the plot would remain undiscovered.

Tudor's pleas to the Almighty proved of little avail. Men known to be servants of Margaret Beaufort were among those taken in arms against their King and her part in encouraging her son to join the rebellion quickly became known to Richard. The King realised that an example must be made in her case, but was anxious to avoid capital punishment where he could. Lord Stanley protested his ignorance of his wife's plotting and pointed to his own loyal attendance on the King throughout his progress, and the number of men his son, Lord Strange had brought from the Stanley estates to serve in the King's army. Accordingly, Richard decreed that Margaret Beaufort should forfeit all her titles and lands, but she would not be named in the Act of Attainder, and her estates would be vested in Lord Stanley for his lifetime. Shortly after, Richard found a replacement for Buckingham in the Office of Constable - this eminent position was given to Thomas, Lord Stanley for his good and loyal service during the rebellion.

John Morton, meanwhile, had made good his escape to Flanders. Like Margaret Beaufort, he was not attainted of high treason, as he had been after Towton, and in view of his absence in secure foreign sanctuary was merely prohibited from the enjoyment of his English properties during the King's pleasure. Once established across the Channel, he lost little time in remaking contact with the Countess of Richmond and with her son, now returned to the Court of Brittany.

The Deceivers had failed in their attempt to overturn Richard's throne by force of arms, but Margaret Beaufort remained the acknowledged head of Lancaster's cause, as another Margaret - Henry VI's Queen - had been before her, and still wielded influence in the Kingdom through her husband's high standing in the King's counsels; Henry Tudor was safe in Brittany and could call on his protector, Duke Francis for support when the times seemed more auspicious; and John Morton, Bishop of Ely, the wiliest plotter in Europe now his French counterpart, Louis XI, was gone, had no more to lose. His own triumphant return to England now depended entirely on a successful invasion by Henry Tudor and he pledged all his long experience, his vast knowledge of the ways of men and their rulers, to the building of a new scheme which, this time, could not fail. It would take the better part of two years before his plans began to bear fruit.

Arms of Henry Stafford, second Duke of Buckingham
The quartering of the Arms of England indicate his
Royal descent through Thomas of Woodstock, youngest son
of Edward III.

CHAPTER ELEVEN

"...on the western coast Rideth a puissant navy;
'Tis thought that Richmond is their admiral..."

At the end of July 1485, a travel-stained rider spurred his horse mercilessly down the road from the East Anglian port of Kings Lynn to Deeping in the Fen country, where Margaret Beaufort anxiously awaited his coming. Reginald Bray was returning from Harfleur, where Henry Tudor was making final preparations for his long-awaited invasion, the last throw of Lancaster. Tudor sent greetings to his mother and bade her send word to supporters of their cause that the true heir to the crown of England would set sail on the first day of August. With him would be John de Vere, Earl of Oxford, veteran of Barnet whence he barely escaped with his life, and now General of Tudor's forces; the Earl of Pembroke, his uncle Jasper Tudor, who led a Welsh army to ruin at Mortimer's Cross, and sundry gentlemen who had fled to France after the debacle of Buckingham's revolt.

Not support to inspire utmost confidence in the success of a desperate enterprise, noted the Lady Margaret, nor would the tatterdemalion army of 2,000 jail-sweepings they led inspire much fear in the hearts of the Yorkist troops they would have to face. But, as her son said through Bray, it was the last chance they would have. John Morton had advised that the French court grew weary of supporting a penniless pretender and was increasingly fearful of Richard's intentions towards their own security. If Lancaster did not strike now, the opportunity would not be given to them a third time. Now or never then, agreed Margaret Beaufort. She must get word to their adherents in the southern counties and in the Southwest and, above all, in South Wales where Henry intended to make his landfall, summoning his fellow Celts to support the self-styled heir of Cadwallader. But the key to the success of the enterprise would be the support of Stanley, her husband, and that of his brother Sir William and, once Bray was rested, he must ride to Nottingham where Lord Stanley, Constable of England, waited on the King and tell him to lose no time in joining her to finalise plans.

Two days later, Thomas Stanley arrived at Deeping and was clearly worried about the prospects for a successful rebellion. He stood high in

Richard's favour, owned broad lands in Lancashire and Cheshire and, as his wife's proxy, in the south and west of the country; he had much to lose if plans went awry. The Lady Margaret poured scorn on his doubts: her son would land with a well-equipped army of 2,000 men at his back and French gold in his purse; all Wales would rise to follow their own and double, nay treble his force; the Woodville faction and the remnants of Lancaster all across England would rise in concert as she had plotted and schemed these two years past and a mighty host would come together and sweep the House of York aside at last.

What could Richard put in the field against them ? His Yorkshiremen and Norfolk's East Anglians. Kent would send no more armies to support him - there would be no plunder to offer from attainted rebels this time - that ditherer Harry Percy might, or might not, bring his Northumbrian levies. London, as ever, would look after its own and the burghers there knew that Richard preferred to spend his time in York or Nottingham. Only the men raised from Cheshire and the Northwest would the King be counting as sure reinforcement - and these were controlled by Stanley and his brother William. There would never be a better time - never another time - to strike. And when the House of Tudor - Lancaster's fresh new sprig - held the crown, uniting the warring Houses of Plantagenet through Henry's marriage to Elizabeth, who would be the greatest Peers in the realm ? The King's step-father and his mother, of course, who would have their pick of the greatest Offices and the richest lands of the Realm.

It was a glowing prospect Margaret Beaufort held out and Stanley warmed to it. He would return to the King in Nottingham and wait there for news of Tudor's landing to reach the court, when Richard was sure to send him post-haste to his estates to raise his forces. Margaret must get word into Wales that he would meet secretly with her son as Tudor's force advanced into England and agree with him the course of action to be followed in the particular circumstances at the time. With this, Margaret had to be content and as she summoned couriers to be ready to ride south and west, Stanley took horse again for Nottingham.

He mused as he rode: to have a grateful King as his step-son would indeed open all doors to him and his family, his future path would be smooth and lined with silk and gold. But - there was ever a 'but' - despite his wife's urgings, the King was a tried and successful warrior with many faithful followers, Tudor was an unknown quantity who had never seen a field of battle. Thomas, second Lord Stanley, had not reached so high a place in

**Traditional portrait of Thomas, Second Lord Stanley,
later Earl of Derby, Step-father of Henry Tudor.**

England's firmament by wagering all on a single throw of the dice. He would take the course he had agreed with his wife, await the King's commission to raise his force, meet with his step-son - for the first time, he reflected - and wait on events. Whatever befell, Stanley would ensure his usual place on the side of the winner. He would move, but slowly, cautiously, and would strike only when it was certain that his blow would be terminal. Thus satisfied with his planned course of action, and inaction, the great trimmer cantered on northwards to Nottingham Castle.

❖   ❖   ❖

Henry Tudor, with 2,000 men, landed in Milford Haven Bay on the southwest tip of Wales during the evening of Sunday August 7th, 1485. He unfurled his Welsh Dragon banner, proclaiming that he had come to retake his kingdom from the usurper Richard Plantagenet, and all true Welshmen were called to join his righteous cause. He appeared an unlikely conqueror: small of build, sallow-skinned, shifty eyes peering suspiciously around, unsmiling, palpably nervous, not a figure to draw a host of followers by the magic of his personality. With him, however, were his uncle Jasper Tudor, who had once commanded much respect in the south of the Principality as half-brother to the anointed King, Henry VI, and John de Vere, Earl of Oxford, who had come closer than most to crushing an army led by Edward IV, when he swept Hastings' wing away at Barnet. Oxford had spent most of his adult life soldiering, fighting in France and other countries during his forced-exile from his native England, and had become one of the most experienced and battle-hardened generals in Europe; his value to the Tudor inheritor of Lancaster's cause would be immense.

The next day, the invaders marched 10 miles north to the nearest town, Haverfordwest, and from here Henry sent messengers to his mother and to the Stanleys in Cheshire asking for the two essentials for his success: men and money. Moving further north to Cardigan and then east to Shrewsbury, which he reached on August 13th, Tudor gathered men along the route with promises of land, offices and plunder. His returning messengers reached him there with money from Margaret Beaufort and news that Sir William Stanley was moving slowly down from Cheshire with a large force while Lord Stanley was between Newport and Stafford also accompanied by many well-armed followers. Anxious to meet with his step-father, Tudor moved quickly forward

Middle and Southern England in the 15th Century

NORTH SEA

IRISH SEA

Richmondes
I.OF MAN
Northallerton
Lancaster · Towton · Yorks
Ripple · Wakefield · Ferrybridge · Ravenspur
Pontefract
Conway
Beaumaris
Rhuddlan · Chester
Carnarvon
Blore Heath
Harlech · Flint · Stoke Field
Shrewsbury · Stafford · Bosworth
Newport · Lichfield · Fotheringhay
Cardigan · Ludlow · Dudley · Kenilworth · Norwich
Mortimers Cross · Warwick · Northampton
Worcester
Haverfordwest · Tewksbury · St Albans · Colchester
Milford Haven · Monmouth · Gloucester · Woodstock · Pleshey Castle
Pembroke · Oxford · Barnet
Bristol · Windsor · London · Rochester · Canterbury
Dover
Winchester · Hastings · Rye · Calais
Southampton · Chichester · Lewes
Portsmouth

ENGLISH CHANNEL

♪ CASTLES

──── HENRY TUDOR'S ROUTE TO BOSWORTH

to Newport, where he had welcome reinforcement from Sir Gilbert Talbot, who brought 500 men to serve under the Dragon banner. Sir Gilbert was son-in-law to the late Lord Hastings and a kinsman of Lady Eleanor Butler whose secret betrothal to Edward IV had disqualified his sons from the succession. The Talbots had little cause to feel affection for the House of York.

Pressing onwards to Stafford, which he reached on August 16th, Tudor found his hoped-for union with Lord Stanley would be further delayed; Stanley had moved south to Lichfield the day before. However, his dashed hopes were raised again when Sir William Stanley arrived with a small escort to assure him that, at the right time, he and his brother would join with the Tudor army and make Henry's path to the throne certain. He recommended that the invading army should turn south to Lichfield, where Lord Stanley had left a quantity of artillery for collection by his step-son, and then proceed via Tamworth towards Leicester, which the usurper Richard had appointed as the rallying point for his army. Somewhere along that route, the Stanleys would rendezvous with Tudor and plans for the final downfall of the Plantagenets would be settled. Encouraged by these promises, but still concerned at the absence of Thomas Stanley, Tudor ordered Oxford to start the army moving south to Lichfield, from where they would swing east again and march to meet Richard's army gathering in Leicester.

Tudor found the artillery he had been promised awaiting him in Lichfield and having collected further supplies, moved on towards Tamworth. Here, messengers from Stanley awaited his arrival to conduct him to the village of Atherstone, a few miles along the road towards Leicester, and here in the darkening evening, Henry Tudor and his step-father met for the first time. Sir William Stanley, who had learned that the King had proclaimed him traitor and set a price on his head, joined their discussion and agreed with Tudor that the three forces should join and advance on Richard's army together. Lord Stanley, however, counselled patience. His son, Lord Strange, was with Richard in Leicester, effectively a hostage for Stanley's loyalty to his King; he dared not risk an open breach at this stage. Instead he proposed the three armies should continue to move separately, his own force to the south and William Stanley's to the north of the path the invaders would take. In this way, they would be ideally located on the flanks of Richard's army when he brought Tudor to battle and could crush him between them.

Henry Tudor, suspicious by nature and unconvinced by Stanley's plan which seemed to him to leave a good deal to chance, nevertheless gave grudging approval. With a small escort, he rode back to his army and told Oxford what had been agreed. To John de Vere, that experienced campaigner, it seemed that, at worst, the Stanleys would not join with Richard's army which could leave him with an advantage in numbers and on that basis he was eager to meet Richard before the King's forces were reinforced further. He would, therefore, commence his final approach towards Leicester the following morning, Saturday August 20th.

Meantime, Thomas Stanley, content with the outcome of his talk with Margaret Beaufort's son, had rejoined his men and ordered a move towards the southeast the next day. Further messages had arrived from Richard during his absence, pressing Stanley to join him at once with all his force and Stanley sent a reply that he would do so and was even now moving towards Leicester. Unhappily his progress was slowed by illness - a sweating sickness had much weakened him - but he was recovering and would be with the King in one or two days at the most. He sent other couriers to Margaret Beaufort at Deeping telling her of the meeting with her son and of their agreed intention to make their separate ways towards the field of battle. In neither message was Stanley specific about which side he would be fighting on when the crunch came, but he was sure the right conclusions would be drawn by the recipients.

Battle-flag of Thomas, second Lord Stanley.

**John Howard, Fifth Duke of Norfolk, killed
in action, Bosworth Field, August 22, 1485**

(Arundel Castle)

CHAPTER TWELVE

"...I have set my life upon a cast
And I will stand the hazard of the die..."

In the evening of August 21st, King Richard's army reached the village of Sutton Cheyney a few miles south of Market Bosworth. Learning from his scouts that Tudor's force was at White Moors, three miles to the southwest of Bosworth, Richard camped for the night in anticipation of a final confrontation with the Pretender the following day. With him Richard had 3,000 bill and pike men and over 1,000 horse brought in by the Earl of Nottingham and Lords Douglas, Scrope, Greystoke and Ferrers. The Duke of Norfolk, John Howard with his son Thomas, Earl of Surrey led a thousand bowmen from East Anglia. Harry Percy, Earl of Northumberland had arrived late, and reluctantly, and his force of some 2,000 spearmen encamped a mile to the rear of the main army. Richard had had reports from York of deliberate tardiness on the part of Northumberland to gather men and obey the royal summons to join the King at Leicester, on which he promised himself to take appropriate action when he had settled with Tudor. For the present, he felt it wisest to leave the men from the north-eastern counties as his rearward.

A further cause for disquiet was the continued absence of Lord Stanley and the movements of his brother, William. Richard's scouts had advised that the two men, with their substantial forces had withdrawn steadily before the advance of the invaders and were currently located to the north and south of his own position. They appeared to be making little effort to join their troops with the King's; it was as if they were watching and waiting on events. Richard knew that he would have to continue to watch them. In light of his uncertainties and knowing the ground well, Richard had decided that early in the morning of August 22nd, he would array his army on the brow of Ambion Hill and await attack by Tudor's force. The invaders had nowhere to go - retreat in the face of Richard's force would be disastrous, his own flanks would be safeguarded by occupation of the high ground and, knowing Oxford's impetuosity from their meeting long before at Barnet, he had little doubt that the shooting star of Lancaster would make a frontal assault uphill, which could be held by his spearmen and cut up by his archers.

Richard's plan of battle would also cater for the more obvious problems which could arise: the possibility of intervention on Tudor's side by the Stanleys from north, south or both, and the questionable loyalties of Harry Percy who would be located in rear of the King's army, with 2,000 men. To cover all these eventualities, Richard located his own cavalry behind his main battle-front where they could keep a watchful eye on Percy to the rear and the Stanley brothers on either flank, and be available to intervene should the need arise. They would also be in position to charge down on Tudor's army as and when the rebel line was broken by his foot and archers. Satisfied with his dispositions, Richard, fully armed and well-mounted, rode with his personal escort of 100 lances to take his chosen position behind the left flank of his front line on the brow of Ambion Hill and looked down towards the southwest, where sunlight glinted on armour and spearpoints and the rumbling murmur of Tudor's approach became steadily louder.

Richard's front, commanded by Norfolk with his son as aide, faced the west; Oxford led his army, now swelled to more than 6,000, towards Ambion from the southwest aiming at the left flank of the force they could see atop the hill, with England's royal banner waving in the forefront. As the column neared the foot of the rise, the advance guard found their horses floundering in ground made marshy by natural springs and sent back to Oxford for orders. John de Vere rode to the front of his halted files and saw further advance by the original route would be potentially disastrous with the ground cutting up badly as horses and men moved across it. Long-experienced in European wars, de Vere saw his only option was to wheel his column to the left and march across the face of Richard's army in order to form a line of battle. This was a dangerous move with the enemy close above him, potentially able to charge down on his flank as his men struggled into position, but he could only see footmen and archers fringing the heights of Ambion, the few horse in evidence were around the Royal Standard. He would take the risk and, without further delay, his Shooting Star banners blowing bravely in the breeze, the Earl of Oxford, veteran Lancastrian, led his whole force steadily across the land at the foot of Ambion Hill.

Richard saw de Vere's manoeuvre from his vantage point and realised the opening it gave him for an immediate attack. But his cavalry was in the wrong place to charge down on his opponent and to bring them forward through his standing lines of infantry must cause chaos all along his front. And what of Northumberland to the rear, or the large groups of heavy cavalry he could see to left and right, watching, waiting, with the Stanley banners flaunting in their midst ? No, this was no time to change a well-made plan. He would hold his position and await Oxford's onset; when this was broken, then and only then, would he lead his horse in the final charge. He sent to Norfolk to hold his ground and await the attack; if Oxford seemed unwilling to advance uphill after his line was formed, then let the bowmen and artillers ply their trade and prick the enemy into close contention as his brother Edward had done years before at Towton. But he knew full well that an opportunity for a quick victory had been missed, and Stanley would pay for its loss once he had settled with Henry Tudor.

At the very rear of the marching column, the Red Dragon of Cadwallader waved over a tight, well-armoured group of horsemen in the midst of which rode the Pretender to the throne of England. Totally unused to warfare, fearful of the approaching conflict, and well aware of the consequences to himself should the coming trial of battle go against him, Henry Tudor had positioned himself as far from the cutting-edge as possible. Well-mounted, he would drive his charger hard for the Welsh border should the day go against him, hoping that the dying of the Frenchmen and Welshmen and English Marchers set between himself and Richard would be prolonged enough to give him a good start towards his native hills.

Unhappily, he noted, the army seemed to have changed its direction of march and now, instead of the long steel-clad file of hardy fighters between him and Richard's army, he found himself just behind the extreme right flank of a line facing uphill towards rank after rank of hard-faced English men-at-arms with, directly above, the Royal Arms displayed over an armoured figure gazing intently down at his army and - it seemed - directly at him. Left to himself, the would-be-king would have quit the field, cursing his mother's pride and ambition for placing him in such peril, vowing vengeance on the Stanleys whose reluctance to stand in his support had left him exposed to the direct onslaught of that fierce, tried warrior Richard Plantagenet. But he was tight-held in the midst of his bodyguard, the ground under their horses' hooves was marshy, clinging, there was no easy escape, no quick, safe route to sanctuary; dry-mouthed, pale-faced, sweating in his heavy casque, Henry Tudor had no course other than to wait the outcome of the battle, which even now was opening with arrows flying and hand-guns belching fire down and up the slopes of Ambion Hill.

Soon, with ammunition on both sides exhausted, the two opposing lines, as if by common consent, lurched towards each other and met in a

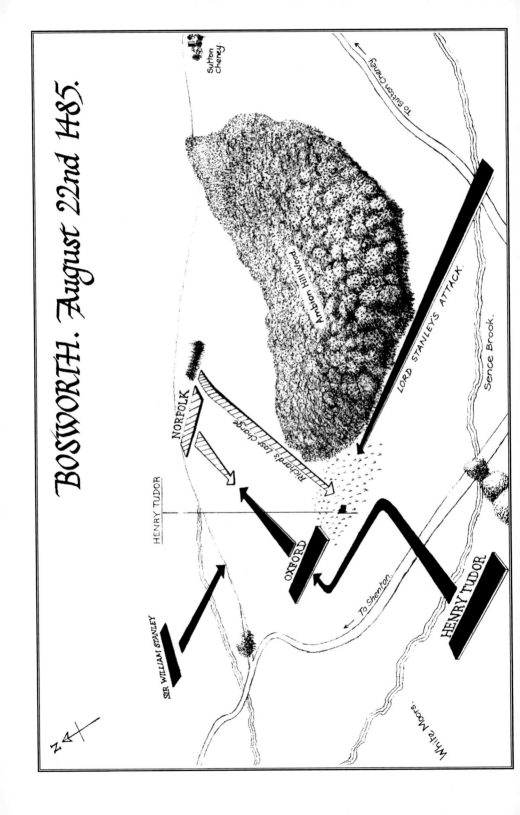

BOSWORTH. August 22nd 1485.

N

Sutton
Cheney.

To Sutton Cheney

Ambion Hill Wood

LORD STANLEY'S ATTACK.

Sence Brook.

NORFOLK

Richard's Last Charge.

HENRY TUDOR

OXFORD

SIR WILLIAM STANLEY

To Shenton.

HENRY TUDOR.

White Moors.

death-grapple mid-way up the slope of Ambion Hill. Both sides realised this was the climax of the fight, there could be no safe retreat from it. Whichever line broke would be decimated and so the men on both sides stood firm to their task trading blow for blow, quarter neither asked nor given. Richard saw a stirring in the cavalry to the north of his line, William Stanley, named as traitor by his King and knowing he could hope for little mercy if the day went against Tudor, urged his men forward at last and attacked Norfolk's right flank. His brother, Tudor's step-father, reluctant still to risk the chance of battle, moved towards the left of Norfolk's line, holding his men in their ranks, waiting - still waiting.

Richard saw Norfolk's line starting to buckle under the new pressure from William Stanley's reinforcement, fresh to the fray, fighting against men already wearied and wounded by more than an hour of close quarter conflict. To his left, Thomas Stanley's force was hovering dangerously, ever-nearing - if his line broke there was no doubt left that Stanley would rush forward to the kill, like a lame, mangy wolf when prey has been weakened by the slashing teeth of the rest of the pack. There was but one throw left: Tudor's standard was below, apart from the conflict raging on the hill. If the Pretender were killed, the head of the rebellion would be cut off, the fight would be purposeless, finished. Richard dropped his visor, raised his battle-axe and shouting to his men to follow, charged down the slope, faster ever faster, and crashed into the armoured group surrounding Henry Tudor.

For a moment it seemed the gamble would succeed, the two groups were broadly equal in numbers and the force of the Yorkist charge threw their opponents back in some disorder. Richard, hacking furiously, killed Tudor's standard bearer and the banner of Cadwallader was stricken to the ground. Sweating, cursing, breathless, the King and his men cut their way forward towards the small panic-stricken figure trying to force a way out of the rear of the brawl, Tudor was nearly within Richard's grasp. But his horse was slipping, stumbling as it tried to find sure footing in the marshy ground ,which had changed the line of Oxford's planned attack, and it fell. The King was pulled to his feet by his esquires who urged him to break off his attack, but he would not.

With a fresh sword in his hand, he raised his hampering visor, shook sweat-drops from his eyes, turned looking for Tudor in the melee, looking, looking, there - no there - where was.... and was struck down. Thomas, Lord Stanley, having seen Richard's fall, believing that Tudor must now gain the day and the crown, had charged into the struggle with all his force and the King with few of his men left was overwhelmed and quickly despatched,

The battle crown which Richard had worn around his casque to identify himself to friend and foe had been struck off in the first clash with Tudor's guard and was found - by the ever-faithful Reginald Bray - safely cushioned amid the clinging twigs of a hawthorn bush, broken and trampled in the last fight of the last of the Plantagenet Kings of England. Taking it, Thomas, Lord Stanley, trimmer, traitor, regicide, placed it on the sweat-matted head of a pallid Henry Tudor, whose shifting eyes were already darting round looking for any seeming less than whole-hearted in their cheering support for his accession to his rightful place on the throne of England.

News of the King's death spread quickly round the field and fighting stopped. With either of the chief protagonists dead, further conflict was purposeless and the killing ended. Too late to save Lord Ferrers, Sir Robert Brackenbury, Constable of the Tower, or Richard's close adviser, Sir Richard Ratclyff, or the faithful John Howard, Duke of Norfolk, who had died among his East Anglians where the fighting had been thickest. Too late for William Catesby, lawyer and legal advisor to the late King, taken in flight and publicly beheaded the following day, despite grovelling – and vain – supplication for mercy to a new monarch, whose first official act had been to order Richard's naked corpse to be dragged by the heels through Leicester and then thrown into an unmarked grave.

Meantime, the new King Henry, seventh monarch of that name and first of the House of Tudor, accepted vows of allegiance from his chief subjects. He bade them welcome to his board, pledged his gratitude for their aid in restoring him to his rights, and sent word to his mother of his triumph and his urgent need for her counsel. She should come to him as soon as he reached London - but first, send to John Morton, whose wise advice had stayed him in his last years of exile, telling him to return home to England to take his deserved place at the King's right hand. King Henry Tudor would have need of him, now more than ever.

Arms of John Howard, Duke of Norfolk.

Henry VII

(Society of Artiquaries of London)

CHAPTER THIRTEEN

"...But if I thrive, the gain of my attempt
The least of you shall share his part thereof..."

The new King, in company with the Earl of Oxford, the Stanleys and many other gentlemen of note, made a triumphant entry into his capital on September 3rd, 1485, twelve days after his victory at Bosworth. He was met at Shoreditch by the Lord Mayor, Aldermen and other dignitaries and rode in a closed carriage to St Paul's where Te Deum was sung in thanksgiving for his victory, in token of which his three battle banners bearing, respectively, St George, Cadwallader's fiery Red Dragon, and a brown cow on a yellow ground were presented and laid up behind the High Altar. Following the service, Henry was escorted to the Bishop of London's Palace where he would lodge for several days.

There, Margaret Beaufort and her son met after more than 15 years of separation. Time had not been kind to her and the travails, trials and tribulations she had endured were clearly marked in the lined face. But, her eyes were still sharp above the high cheekbones, the same watchful expression ever-present, and the small, thin figure still stiffly upright in evidence of her pride in the blood-royal which flowed so copiously in her veins. The two knelt and gave thanks together for their great deliverance and sat to talk of what was still to do to buttress the House of Tudor's rule over England.

John Morton had written from Flanders, where he was settling his affairs, thanking God that the right had prevailed, and expecting to be in London in a few days. His wise council would be invaluable to them and his great service to their House, and to Lancaster, would be recognised and recompensed. In his letter, he pressed three immediate steps to be taken: the King should summon the members of his Great Council to meet as soon as he reached London, and they be required to start arrangements for an early coronation, followed by his marriage to Elizabeth of York. With the date fixed for his formal crowning, the King should look to summon his first Parliament within a week to provide the necessary legislative foundation for the continuing rule of the Tudor line. Henry nodded as he read, Morton's thinking was, as ever, clear and to the point - the only omission was that England must have a new Chancellor of proven loyalty to the new monarch, and Henry Tudor knew who that man must be. So, for that matter, did John Morton.

Henry would set the programme in train in the morning and would decide then what rewards might be given to those who had helped in the recovery of his throne. Clearly, the first Act of his Parliament must be to reverse all Yorkist Attainders, thus restoring lands and titles to their rightful, Lancastrian owners. His dear mother would have full rights again in her own properties and she must keep close to him as her wise counsel was essential to his success. He realised this would leave her less time to act in a supportive role to her husband but, after all the years of forced-separation, as her only son, and King, he must insist on her continual presence, at least in the early years of his rule.

Naturally, he would reward his step-father in appropriate measure for the risks he had taken in supporting his rightful claims - he had it in mind to create him Earl of Derby, the old Lancastrian title held by Henry IV, which would surely be gratifying to Lord Stanley, and Buckingham's former post as Constable would also be his. His brother, Sir William, could have the Lord Chamberlain's Office, held for so many years by Hastings under the usurper Edward. Appropriate, perhaps, that Stanleys should take Offices held by men who had died as a direct result of their scheming. The King half-smiled at the thought and the ever-shifting eyes looked to see whether his mother had grasped the same point.

As to land, that could be dealt with later perhaps - he had already given the spoils of the battlefield over to Lord Thomas and Sir William, which would be enough for the present. The Stanleys had been late in their intervention at Bosworth - dangerously late. He might have been killed had they delayed longer. Henry paled again at the memory of that oncoming figure in scratched, dinted armour, clasping a bloody axe, eyes fixed unwaveringly on him. He shuddered inwardly - the Stanleys must wait on his decisions now, as he had had to wait on theirs

For his Uncle Jasper though, who had shared his long exile after Tewkesbury, a grander title: Duke of Bedford, say, like the brother of great Harry V; Oxford would have his titles and lands restored when the old Attainders were revoked and the Courtenays should be confirmed as Earls of Devon. There were so many others, some more worthy some less, but he could leave all these details to Morton. For himself, he intended to take all the lands and revenues held by Henry VI prior to First St Albans and he knew he could rely on his new Chancellor to ensure that future provisions by Parliament were adequate to England's new King ruling with regal dignity over a land with well-financed defences against its enemies. The days of penury, loans, remittances, begging, were over. He would be England's richest King and ensure that his dues were always paid promptly, and to the last farthing.

He wished Morton would get here quickly - his King had great need of his services. Margaret Beaufort was sure the good Bishop would be with them in a few days. He had never yet disappointed her nor deserved less than her good opinion. His service to their cause had been invaluable. Soon, Henry, he will come soon. Comforted as in days long gone, by his mother's calm assurances, the King of England led her out to join the company for supper.

The first meeting of Henry VII's Great Council took place the following week at Westminster and set October 30th as the date on which their new, undoubted King would be crowned. Arrangements would be made to bring Elizabeth of York from Sheriff Hutton in preparation for the royal wedding which was scheduled for mid-January in the New Year, and a summons was sent out to Parliamentary members to the first meeting of the new reign on November 7th - all in line with the recommendations of the Grey Eminence, en route home from Flanders. The King also gave indications of the titles which would be bestowed on his supporters, including the thought that, in due time, a hard-earned K.G. should be bestowed on Reginald Bray at the insistence of the greatest Lady in the land, Margaret Beaufort, Mother to his Grace.

With Morton returned, all arrangements slotted logically into place. The Coronation took place at the prescribed time and, in November, Henry's first Parliament obediently reversed all Yorkist Acts of Attainder - simultaneously attainting of Treason the surviving leaders of the party of York, and, most importantly, decreed "that the inheritance of the crown should rest, remain and abide in the King". Thus the throne of England was entailed to the House of Tudor, without mention of their right being by conquest nor by virtue of the line of succession through Henry's intended wife, Elizabeth. A most subtle piece of legislation, worthy of the crafty brain which formulated the wording.

On January 18th of the following year, the eldest daughter of Edward IV duly married Henry Tudor amid scenes of surpassing splendour, pomp and rejoicing. Red rose and White were united in the new Tudor emblem; the warring Houses of Plantagenet were subsumed - in outward appearance at least - in the new Dynasty. More significantly, perhaps, on March 6th following, John Morton was appointed Chancellor of England and a month later, on the death of Thomas, Cardinal Bourchier, was designated Archbishop of Canterbury, in which high Office he was formally enthroned on January 28th, 1487. The humble Parson of Blokesworth was become ecclesiastical leader of his country, chief Civil Servant and adviser to the King, and friend and counsellor to the King's Mother. Rich indeed were the rewards of virtue, of mediaeval meritocracy, and of murderous conspiracy.

Others were less surfeited with good things. Thomas, Lord Stanley had the Earldom of Derby for himself and his heirs, but his estates were little greater, indeed with the reversion of the Beaufort and Holland lands to his wife's direct control and ownership, he could be adjudged to be somewhat worse off. Furthermore, the Lady Margaret did not see her main role in life as Countess of Derby - rather was she the King's Mother, duty-bound to be ever-available in the service of her beloved son and to ensure this had legally taken the status of Femme Sole, to be followed by a vow of chastity, all of which left Stanley married to her but without conjugal rights. He consoled himself by turning again to aesthetic pursuits amongst the fruits of which was an epic poem, in the Romantic style, on Bosworth and the tragic death of King Richard.

Arms and signature of Reginald (Reynald) Bray KG.

89

CHAPTER FOURTEEN

"...Abate the edge of traitors, gracious Lord,
That would reduce these bloody days again..."

The first full year of the reign of the House of Tudor was not without incident. Angry risings in Cornwall and Yorkshire had to be put down with force and many embers of resentment were left smouldering, waiting only the blast of a fresh Yorkist wind to fan them into flame again. Early in January 1487, John Morton's information sources in Ireland advised of a new threat to the peace of the Kingdom, which the Archbishop of Canterbury-elect felt were serious enough to bring to the attention of his royal master and the Lady Margaret Beaufort, Countess of Derby and Richmond.

The three met in the King's private chambers at Westminster, where Morton revealed that a personable young man had appeared in Dublin claiming to be Edward, Earl of Warwick, son of George of Clarence and thereby nearest male heir to the Yorkist claim to the crown. According to Morton's informants, the claim had the backing of Margaret of Burgundy, elder sister of Richard III and was likely to be supported by John de la Pole, Earl of Lincoln, who had been designated heir to Richard's throne before Bosworth. Henry Tudor was angered by the news; when would these Yorkist usurpers cease to trouble him ? And at such a time as this, when all thoughts should be on the religious implications of the enthronement of a new Archbishop, now only days away. And again, the real Edward of Warwick was housed in the Tower - how could an impostor hope to pass himself off as a man Henry had kept in close custody since he retook his throne from the usurper Richard ? It was impossible, not a soul would believe it.

His mother and Morton calmed their agitated King. It was early days certainly and perhaps this new plot would fizzle out as the earlier troubles had. If it did not, then John de Vere - under the watchful eye of his King, naturally - would surely prove equal to dealing with the problem and, meantime, as news of the imposture spread, it might be politic to have the true Edward paraded with some pomp through London, to let the people see for themselves the lie on which the Yorkist schemes was based. Nervous wrath cooling somewhat under the soothing hands of his mother and the quiet, logic of Morton, Henry agreed with his advisers on the course to be pursued immediately, and the thoughts of the trio were turned to happier things, pre-eminently the elevation of the Bishop of Ely to the throne of Canterbury.

Events followed an untroubled course for some months after Morton's ascent to the highest office in England's Church but, by the end of May it became clear that warclouds were again gathering in the early Summer skies. News came that, on May 24th, the Pretender had been crowned as Edward VI in Dublin and joined by Lincoln and Francis, Lord Lovell, a former intimate of Richard III's and survivor of Bosworth. More important than the comparatively few English soldiers with the Yorkist nobles were the 2,000 well-equipped German troops under command of one Martin Schwartz, an experienced mercenary-leader hired by Margaret of Burgundy. Several thousand Irishmen under the Earl of Kildare had also attached themselves to the Yorkist cause and the whole army was transported to the Lancashire coast, landing on June 4th, 1487.

Hastily summoning his war-leaders, the Earl of Oxford and his uncle, Jasper Tudor, now Duke of Bedford, Henry ordered a concentration at Nottingham within 10 days and on the evening of June 14th the King sat down there in his predecessor's "Castle of Care", for a Council of War with Oxford, Bedford and the young Lord Strange, son of Thomas Stanley, who had joined the royal force with 6,000 well-armed men under the banner of the King's stepfather. Stanley was not a man to hesitate at choosing sides in a fight between thousands of well-found English troops and a rabble of Irish with a stiffening of Germans - nor could he look for mercy at the hands of Lincoln and Lovell in the event of a Yorkist victory. However, he himself was ageing and infirm and felt his son and heir would be capable of serving his King better in the field; Stanley would await the joyous tidings of his stepson's inevitable victory, which would surely help rouse him from his present bed of sickness and pain. Henry Tudor's thin lips tightened at this news, but he knew by now who his true friemds were and it would not be expedient to quarrel with Lord Strange as leader of the largest single contingent in his force. One day perhaps, there would be time for an accounting with the Stanleys, but not yet - not quite yet.

Oxford's scouts had located the enemy encamped a dozen miles to the northeast of the King's army in and around the village of Southwell. Indications were that the Yorkists were making towards Newark hoping, probably, to slip past Henry's army and take the Great North Road south to London. John de Vere, ever-eager to bring his foes to battle proposed that the army should form in three fighting divisions rather than in column of march and move steadily towards Lincoln's force with a view to crushing them against the River Trent. This was agreed and, as a mark of his favour, Henry gave command of the vanguard to Oxford reserving for himself the main, centre division, with Bedford bringing up the small rearguard.

On Friday, June 15th, the Tudor army set out northeastwards up the Fosse Way from Nottingham, travelling as arranged in three divisions each arrayed for battle. The formations proving more cumbersome in practice than in planning, made only slow progress towards their goal and Henry called a halt for the night still several miles short of Newark. Meantime, the Earl of Lincoln, aware of the royal army's movement had positioned his forces along a ridge crossing the Fosse Way a mile south of a village called East Stoke and between Newark and the oncoming heirs of vanished Lancastrian armies. The last confrontation between White Rose and Red would be fought on June 16th, 1487 and History would name it Stoke Field.

Early that morning, the armies roused and Oxford led his division forward up the slope facing him, as he had done at Bosworth two year earlier, and closed with his opponents. Lincoln, whose strength was based entirely on his disciplined German mercenaries kept them in a solid grouping holding the centre while attacking Oxford's flanks with his wild, ill-armed Irish levies. The German core held their ground well and, with the Gaelic berserkers making progress around the flanks the fight quickly developed into a desperate slogging match, a wild brawl which seemed progressively likely to engulf the Tudor vanguard completely.

Henry Tudor watched Oxford's struggle from the safety of the centre of his well-armoured centre division, which was still some way off from the fight having advanced more slowly than Oxford's men. When urged by his captains of the need to follow more closely, Henry had told them that Oxford would do well enough and could probably settle the fight himself. What support could the veteran of Barnet and Bosworth need against a handful of Germans and a rabble-in-arms from the peat bogs ? And what was he doing here, again imprisoned in hot heavy armour, sweat stinging his eyes, in peril of his life ? Was this how a King of England was supposed to live? Let de Vere earn his pay and his place as the King's General, let him break his King's enemies, and then the survivors would pay dearly for their affront to his royal dignity.

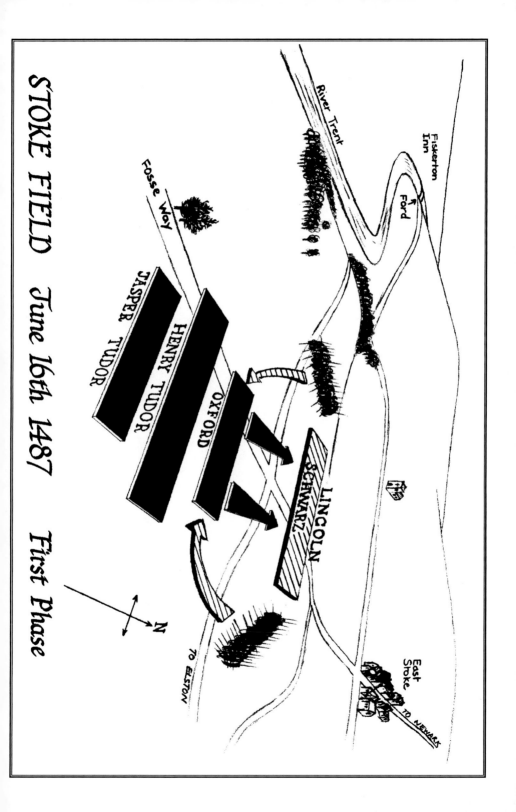

STOKE FIELD   June 16th 1487   First Phase

But as the fight before them ended a second hour, with no sign of Oxford breaking through, Henry ordered his leading files to move forward to the attack, while he continued to watch and wait from the safety of the rearmost line. Re-invigorated by the arrival of the reinforcement, John de Vere urged his men to a final effort and, with the centre crumbling and the wild, unarmoured Irishmen starting to look behind for a road to safety, the Yorkist line dissolved and broke in flight. As at Towton and Tewkesbury years before, the fugitives found themselves on the wrong side of a water-barrier and many hundreds died. The Earl of Lincoln fell in the centre of the battle, together with Schwarz and his Germans, who earned their pay in full. The Pretender, a mere youth named Lambert Simnel was captured and, to mark his insignificance, was set to work as a turnspit in the King's kitchens.

The royal army advanced triumphantly to Lincoln, capturing many more fugitives en route and these were hanged in the city's ancient streets. Francis Lovell, as at Bosworth, had made good his escape from the stricken field and reached his ancestral home at Minster Lovell. The King's men found him here, hiding in the cellars, and on royal orders, walled up the exits and left him to die of starvation. Thus perished miserably the last of Richard III's "band of brothers" from his happiest days at Middleham. Henry Tudor having made the rebels pay for their temerity in threatening his throne, and his very life, returned to London to receive the plaudits of his people and the comforting praise of his ever-loving mother. England, and his throne and, above all, his own person, were safe. The Good God, to whom Te Deums of thanksgiving were raised at St Paul's yet again, would surely grant that this would be the last time King Henry Tudor must venture his safety on the fortune of battle.

Returned from the celebrations and services of thanksgiving, the King sat with his mother and his Lord Chancellor in his chambers at Westminster. He felt at peace with the world and with Lincoln and Lovell dead it seemed reasonable to assume that his troubles were at an end. Margaret Beaufort and John Morton exchanged a meaningful glance, the Countess nodded and Morton cleared his throat preparatory to speaking. Henry Tudor, immediately sensing new revelations of unquiet yet to come, sat forward, tense again, eyes nervously shifting from one to the other, and demanded to know what further problem could possibly have arisen. Morton suggested that his mother was best equipped in this particular case to relate what had happened, since it involved her directly.

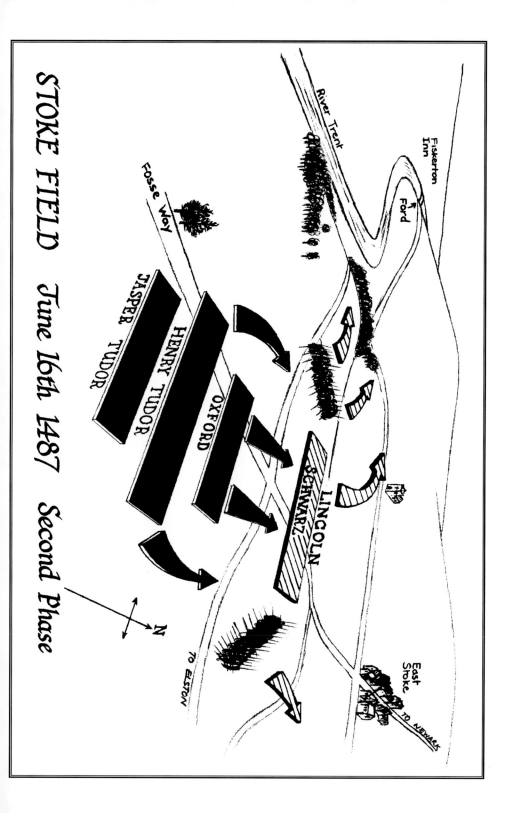

STOKE FIELD   June 16th 1487   Second Phase

River Trent

Fosse Way

Fiskerton Inn

Ford

JASPER TUDOR

HENRY TUDOR

OXFORD

LINCOLN

SCHWARZ

N

TO ELSTON

East Stoke

TO NEWARK

Margaret Beaufort told her son that evidence had come to light indicating that the Simnel conspiracy had involved one other highly placed person, to wit : the King's mother-in-law, Elizabeth Woodville. Some months before, the Dowager-Queen had asked for a meeting with the Lady Margaret and, during their talk, had chided the King's mother for interfering in arrangements which were properly the responsibility of the new Queen Elizabeth. One thing had led to another, the exchanges had become progressively angrier, until Margaret Beaufort had ordered Elizabeth Woodville to say no more, lest she deal with her as she had with her sons years before. Stunned, the former Queen demanded to know what she meant - King Richard himself had told her that Buckingham alone was responsible for their deaths - and then, with dawning comprehension, she had said that Morton was there at Brecknock, and hurried out clearly distressed.

John Morton took up the account. It appeared that she had subsequently taken steps to use her influence, covertly, in favour of Simnel and he was sure the King would see that this was a matter demanding urgent attention. He would suggest that the former Queen might be lodged, permanently, in the nunnery at Bermondsey where the Sisters could be told that Elizabeth Woodville had had enough of the material world and had taken a vow of perpetual silence. The King agreed immediately; for his mother's sake Edward's ingrate widow must be sent where she could do no more harm and the lands he had bestowed for her upkeep would naturally return to the royal demesne. Let the matter be put in hand without delay - the name of Elizabeth Woodville should be included among those condemned for conspiracy in the next Parliament.

And, lest this should stir up trouble among Woodville remnants, it would be timely to commence planning for the crowning of his own Queen Elizabeth, which must take place before the Christmas feast - Morton should see to it. Now, let there be no more talk of such things; the King must relax, he had had a very tiring campaign and needed rest above all things. Henry Tudor sat quietly, musing over the unexpected increase in his income which had just emerged from his mother-in-law's treachery, his feelings of contentment progressively returning, his ever-loyal, ever-loving mother by his side. Peace and plenty were indeed the most desirable of all things.

CHAPTER FIFTEEN

"...Enrich the time to come with smooth-fac'd peace,
With smiling plenty, and fair prosperous days !..."

After two years of peace, King Henry's thoughts had turned again to war. Not to the sudden shock of risky battle - God forbid - but to the profitability of campaigning in another land. He had chided John Morton at their regular meeting in his palace of Westminster with the parlous state of the royal finances. Yes, yes, he had land and wealth and Parliament and the Church granted their regular tenths, but it was not enough. It would never be enough. He saw wealth on every hand as he rode about his capital city and through the peaceful lands of his realm - peace which he, the King, mark you - had given to the land, and his own reward was paltry by comparison.

Morton agreed with his monarch. The country had not repaid his wise governance as it ought, but the raising of new taxation was ever a risky business and could cause civil commotion which usually proved costly to the King's Treasury. A better way might be to emulate his late father-in-law, Edward and revive England's claims to the throne of France. The people were ever-eager for French campaigns which brought much wealth to the country without the many unpleasantnesses connected with civil war in their own land. During King Edward's reign, he had assisted in the inception and collection of Benevolences - a special tax by which lords and people could show their love for their King, through contributing to his war-chest for a venture into France. The practice had been discontinued by the usurper Richard, but his Acts in no way bound the new, rightful King.

Morton had found that Benevolences, when properly and firmly pressed, tended to produce more money than was really needed for a campaign and the yield could be augmented very substantially through a clever ploy, whereby those who made a great show of their wealth could be pressed to make large contributions to their King's coffers, and those who lived poorly were obviously careful of their moneys and therefore must have much gold laid up, which, surely, they would wish to share with their monarch. The final coup came when, having put an army into France,

England's King could negotiate with the French court - and the King of France was still but a boy - for an armistice or truce and there was little doubt that France would pay handsomely for the English force to return home, where it could be quickly disbanded, keeping pay to a minimum.

Henry Tudor liked what he heard, the inflow of funds to the royal coffers would be enormous. And, of course, his claim to the French throne through his direct descent from Edward III was unquestionable and, again, he had not always been comfortable during his years of exile in Brittany or in France. There had been times when his very life had been threatened by one side or the other, as Morton reminded him. Yes, an armed excursion to France could be an enjoyable expedition, but it must be well provisioned in every way. Let his Chancellor ensure that ample funds were available for the venture, which should be undertaken, say, no later than the Summer or early Autumn of 1492. The King left the chamber and John Morton, still limber despite his 70 years, hurried to his own Palace to confer with Sir Reginald Bray on the revival of a Benevolence with dual prongs.

A subsidy for King Henry's projected war with France was granted by the third Parliament of his reign and, within weeks, couriers rode out the length and breadth of the land bearing orders signed by the King, requiring his Lieutenants in every county to call for and collect the new benevolences which would be used to finance the pursuit of their monarch's rightful claim to the throne of France. Collection of the new tax did not go as smoothly as Morton had hoped, particularly in Yorkshire and Durham, where King Richard had enjoyed his greatest popularity. Instead, riotous assemblies formed in many towns and Henry Percy, now Duke of Northumberland, and Lieutenant for the northeastern counties, felt obliged to write to his King suggesting some amelioration.

An angry response from King Henry included strong threats of action if the due taxes were not paid to the uttermost farthing and Percy, hoping to minimise his own involvement in the quarrel, read the King's letter to an already angry crowd of Yorkshire townsmen in Thirsk. Infuriated by the response and the explicit threats contained, the gathering of protesters became a lynch-mob on the instant, dragged the hapless Percy from his horse and killed him. Four years after his laggard support at Bosworth had contributed largely to the death of the last Yorkist King, Harry Percy had sharp justice at the hands of Yorkshiremen. His son, the young Henry Percy, wrote sadly to the King to tell him of the mischance to his father, brought about by his fidelity to his monarch's commands. Henry Tudor replied that any man fool enough to utter threats - albeit written by his King - to an angry mob deserved what befell him, and the new Duke should note that he must pay a fine of £10,000 to the King in lieu of the tax his late father had failed so lamentably to collect.

Some three years after this untoward event, Henry Tudor, in course of leisurely besieging Boulogne during October, received ambassadors from Charles of France proposing negotiations, much as John Morton had predicted. Peace was speedily concluded by the Treaty of Etaples, signed on November 6th, 1492, whereby the King of England received a lump sum of £ 127,000 to cover his expenses, plus a yearly pension of £ 6,000, and agreed to withdraw his army from France. The English negotiators amongst whom Morton again played a leading role also received generous largesse for their efforts and all returned to London where, after a triumphal celebration of the King's prowess in arms, the army was swiftly disbanded.

In addition to his largesse, John Morton, Archbishop of Canterbury, Chancellor of England was, in the year following, created Cardinal of St Anastasia by His Holiness the Pope at the urgent prayer of that most puissant monarch, Henry, by the Grace of God, King of England and Ireland, but not - tacitly - of France.

The negotiations at Etaples included some discussion of a new Pretender to the English crown, who had appeared in Ireland a year or so previously and made a good impression among the Irish gentry. His name was Perkin Warbeck and, though raised in Flanders, his claim to be Edward IV's second son, Richard of York was more credible than Lambert Simnel's personation of Edward of Warwick. Following Henry Tudor's declaration of war against France, Charles VIII invited Warbeck to his court in Paris, where he was well received, but after the Treaty had been signed, he was asked to move on to Burgundy, where the Duchess Margaret was happy to welcome a new potential threat to Henry VII's quiet enjoyment of his throne.

When reports of Warbeck's activities in Ireland first reached the court, Henry had been dismissive of their importance. After the examples made, following the Simnel episode, it was unlikely - to say the least - that

**Traditional Portrait of Sir William Stanley
"the richest commoner in England".**

Englishmen of any consequence would be likely to take up this new cause. Let the fool, whoever he was, run round among the Irish bogs looking for support; he and they would soon tire of that sport and Warbeck would disappear back into the mists he had emerged from. John Morton agreed with his King, but made a mental note to keep a watchful eye on any possible developments within the Kingdom. He had not risen so high by overlooking details, however minor they appeared.

Morton's foresight was to prove accurate for, within a year of the profitable expedition into France, his spies had identified a growing number of English gentlemen who were in covert correspondence with Burgundy including Lord Fitzwalter, Sir Robert Clifford, Sir Simon Mountfort and Sir Thomas Thwaites. The Chancellor increased surveillance of the growing conspiracy and was able to infiltrate selected men into the councils of the plotters. These informants gathered intelligence indicating involvement of Lords of high standing at the court of Philip, Count of Flanders, son of the Emperor Maximillian, and son-in-law of Margaret of Burgundy; Charles of France - unsurprisingly - was increasingly sympathetic to Warbeck's cause, and a further, important name was added to the list of English plotters. Under questioning, several plotters had revealed that Sir William Stanley, Lord Chamberlain and the King's uncle by marriage, had indicated that if - as seemed increasingly likely - Perkin Warbeck was indeed the son of Edward IV, then he would not bear arms against him

His signature "Stanley Chamberlain".

CHAPTER SIXTEEN

"...the extreme peril of the case,
The peace of England and our persons' safety,
Enforc'd us to this execution..."

William Stanley had made little effort to hide his discontent with the slimness of his rewards in the new reign. The Office of Lord Chamberlain was well enough, but bore with it few perquisites, and the additional grant of a couple of Manors hardly provided the wherewithal to finance the lifestyle of one who had placed King Henry Tudor on his throne. For years after Bosworth, Stanley's resentment at the royal ingratitude had grown and when his petition that he be granted the ancient title of Earl of Chester, was sharply rejected by Henry on grounds that this honour was reserved for the royal house alone, Sir William - like Harry Hotspur and Richard Neville before him - cursed the base ingratitude of man-made Kings. Like them, he mused that Kings could be pulled down as well as set up and perhaps it was time for William Stanley to find a more generous royal patron.

John Morton lost no time in bringing this fruit of his intelligence-gathering to Henry Tudor's notice. The King was not pleased with the news. A fine way to start the New Year - a new nest of traitors and, joined with them, his own mother's brother-in-law. Well, William Stanley could look for no mercy on that account; let him be arrested, brought to trial and executed with Fitzwalter and the rest. The Stanleys had always been grudging in their support, they had been laggard in coming to his aid at Bosworth, in fact the battle was all but decided by his own - and Oxford's - efforts before the brothers saw fit to make their allegiance clear. And then there was this affair of his asking for the Chester Earldom - what impudence ! Did the man pretend to the blood-royal ? Let the headsman see the colour of his blood, the King had had enough of Sir William Stanley.

Morton agreed, indeed he had anticipated the King's wishes and arrangements were already in hand. Stanley was arrested later that day, questioned and brought to trial; Henry's judges heard the reports on Stanley's statement - which Sir William did not deny - and despite his arguments to the contrary, held that there was no such thing in Law as "conditional Treason".

The Lord Chamberlain was condemned as a traitor and on February 16th 1495 paid the price on the headsman's block. His worldly goods were seized for the King and it was found that, contrary to his complaints of comparative poverty, Stanley had died a very rich man. Thus, ironically, the profits from betraying the last Yorkist King went, in the end, as part-payment for the adjudged betrayal of his successor. In the Summer of that year, at his mother's urging, Henry Tudor spent some weeks at leisure with her and Thomas Stanley at their seat at Lathom in Lancashire, making clear that his stepfather was in no way involved in the Warbeck plot.

Unhappily, hardly was this idyllic interlude concluded than news came of an attempted landing in Kent by a small fleet under Warbeck's command. This was unsuccessful and the handful of Warbeck's men who had gained the shore were brought to London and publicly hanged. Not to be discouraged, Warbeck sailed west to Ireland, where his forces besieged Waterford, before being beaten off and taking to the sea again, this time making north to Scotland, where the Pretender was royally received by King James IV. Yet again, the King of England must summon up his nerve and spend his treasure to assure continued occupation of the throne he had himself usurped. And his nerves were stretching progressively thin, and he hated wasting treasure on keeping what was rightfully his by his royal descent. He summoned his Chancellor to meet with him and his mother at Westminster.

It was cold even in the King's private apartments that December day of 1495 and the three sitting at the table were heavily shrouded in thick, woollen gowns trimmed with fur. Henry Tudor looked up from the report in front of him, his mouth distorting in anger, it was insufferable - Warbeck received by the King of Scotland, in Stirling as lately as November 26, and promising treasure and the cession of Berwick if James would join with his enterprise into England. What treasure had Warbeck, other than that he expected to steal from Henry, and by what right did he cede land to the Scots? Had half the rulers of Europe gone mad ? He could understand James, all Scots were Border-reivers at heart, and that Yorkist bitch Margaret of Burgundy, still plotting against the true heirs of Lancaster, and Charles of France, still sore from the payments he had been forced to make at Etaples. But the Emperor, and his son Philip of Flanders, how could they be so deceived by this mountebank, this impostor, as to support his claims.

The Cardinal Archbishop, as always, had soothing words for his King. It was as Henry had described it: Burgundy sought revenge for Bosworth and Stoke Field, France was always glad to see trouble stirred across the Channel, to reduce the possibility of attacks on their own lands, and the Scots had an insatiable appetite for raiding into England's northern counties for which the thinnest of excuses was good enough. As for the Emperor, his son was now son-in-law to Margaret of Burgundy and the Duchess had doubtless impressed her new relatives with her own belief, so-called, in Warbeck's identity as her nephew Richard of York.

Margaret Beaufort raised her hooded eyes from the report her son had passed to her. All that the Archbishop had said was true, but there seemed to be more to the affair than the desire of other rulers to see England weakened, or to seize plunder and advantage from a new roiling of English politics. She had heard of men she would consider honest - fools, but in their way honest - who had accepted Warbeck's claim to be the second son of Edward IV. How could this be possible ? Morton looked across at the thin, shrewd face, much-lined in the service of her House and her son, the Lady Margaret had placed her finger on the single, real reason for disquiet in the whole matter. Warbeck was a play-actor, a counterfeit, a liar - he was no more Richard of York than he was Edward V - but well-founded reports from his agents in Flanders indicated that there was a solitary grain of truth at the centre of Warbeck's lie: it was very probable that he was a son of Edward IV, a by-blow from Edward's stay in Flanders before his triumphant return to Barnet and Tewkesbury. Hence his success in passing himself off as Richard, the young Duke of York.

Morton's thunderbolt struck Henry Tudor almost as a physical blow. The King rose from his seat and strode around the chamber, the small figure tensed within the swaddling gown, sallow face pale, long thin fingers clasping and loosing the fur trimming around his shoulders. It was bad enough that this impostor should be leaguing himself with that Scots thief, James and his horde of plunderers, but that he should truly have Edward's blood in his veins - bastard or not - was infinitely more dangerous. Let him get into Yorkshire, among Richard's men, and all north England could be ablaze again in an instant, and then East Anglia, Kent, the Midlands. Where would it stop - could it be stopped ?

Henry Tudor slumped back into his chair, his mother went to him, calming, consoling this her son whom she had never been able to mother in

Margaret Beaufort by Rowland Lockey

(St. John's College, Cambridge)

his childhood and youth. All would be well, Oxford was still their staunch general and Surrey, Norfolk's son, now released from the Tower was grateful for Henry's mercy and would surely wish to demonstrate his loyalty against the Scots. The three of them knew well that Warbeck - Plantagenet blood or none - was a Pretender and therefore it was impossible he should succeed in his wild venture. Henry looked up at her standing by his chair, standing before him against the world if needs be, like an old vixen fierce in defence of her last cub, and shook his head. It was very well that they knew Warbeck's tale to be false, but how could they prove it to the world out there. They could not parade the real Richard of York through London as they had Edward of Warwick years before to show up the lies of Simnel. Much less could they reveal the real fate of the two brothers and who had been involved in their....his voice trailed off; he could not bring himself to mouth the word.

John Morton, having waited for the storm of regal anger to abate, cleared his throat. It seemed to him that there might be one solution to the problem of revealing Warbeck's tale to be the lie it was if his King would care to hear it. His King nodded, the crafty eyes moving over the plump, pink face of the Primate of All England, Margaret Beaufort likewise awaited the solution from the one man who had never failed her or her cause.

It was quite simple really said England's Chancellor. The two boys were dead. They were killed by Buckingham for good and sufficient reasons which there was no profit in exploring now, and it would be impolitic to make such a revelation at this stage, when people would still remember in whose support Buckingham had subsequently rebelled and died, and other details such as who his close relations were and who had been his prime confidant before and at the time of the revolt. However, the news must come out if Warbeck's claims were to be set at naught and so they must employ the rumour, the whispered confidence, the all-knowing wink-and-nod which he could do through a veritable grape-vine of agents in London and through the country.

For maximum effect, the rumour must be based largely in actual truth and combined with one great untruth. The story his men would put about would be that the Princes were murdered on the orders of their uncle, King Richard to ensure his tenure of England's throne. The account should be elaborated sufficiently to encourage acceptance of its authenticity, that was the best method. It might be possible to implicate some former subordinate of the dead usurper, for example – a senior captain perhaps. Not Buckingham –

that would bring the story too near the truth for safety. He would have to give this a deal of thought. But what did His Majesty think of the essential idea?

Margaret Beaufort and her son looked at each other in silence and then away, eyes running over Morton's seraphic face and away again, half-unwilling to contemplate the evil so clearly and logically explored, but accepting its compelling force as an answer to the threat to their high place. The King asked Morton if he was sure it could be done and his Chancellor re-assured him: give him a few weeks only and his whispering campaign would have established that Edward's sons were dead and that Richard and some of his minions were responsible for their passing. If His Grace pleased, he would set to work on the project immediately - he had a new, young clerk, one Thomas More, whose name he had mentioned to the King before as one who would go far. He would dictate a memorandum of events to More and then circulate copies to his agents with instructions as to its dissemination. Naturally, with the King's and Lady Margaret's agreement....

Henry nodded at last, let it be done. He crossed himself and prayed that God would have mercy on the soul of that murdering usurper Richard, last of the Plantagenets. Margaret Beaufort said Amen. She and her son were ever-dutiful children of the Holy Catholic Church.

Signature of Richard III when Duke of Gloucester, and his motto: Loyaulte me lie - "Loyalty bindeth me".

*Sir Reginald Bray KG, from a stained glass window
in Great Malvern Priory.*

EPILOGUE

"...Now civil wounds are stopp'd, peace lives again -
That she may long live here, God say amen !..."

Perkin Warbeck, bastard son of Edward IV, duly accompanied an invading rag-tag army of Scottish Borderers in September 1496, which robbed and ravaged much of Northumberland, before retiring into their own land again on the approach of an English force. Finding no prospect of further help from James IV, Warbeck tried his luck again the following year in Cornwall, where there had been strife and rebellion due to the activities of the King's tax gatherers, culminating in a battle at Blackheath, in which the ever-faithful John de Vere, Earl of Oxford had conquered again in Henry's name. At the same time, Thomas Howard, Earl of Surrey, redeemed his family's name with the new ruler by leading a successful punitive expedition against the Scots. Running out of supporters, Warbeck surrendered to the King's mercy in October 1497, was imprisoned in the Tower for two years and executed on 23rd November, 1499.

John Morton, Cardinal Archbishop of Canterbury, Chancellor of England and the King's most faithful adviser, died full of years as the century turned and was buried in his Cathedral at Canterbury. In his will he left ample funds for the support of poor scholars at Oxford and Cambridge, a gold breviary to his royal master and a portraiture of Our Lady in pure gold to Lady Margaret, Countess of Richmond. The residue of his estate was left to his nephews Thomas and John Morton, after payment of 1,000 marks for his funeral expenses and after the Bishopric of Ely had engaged to pray for his soul's salvation every day for 20 years after his demise. "Thus died in the Lord this worthy father of great years...he had served three kings....and was renowned for piety, wit, learning and experience." An alternative and briefer epitaph stated that "In this year (1500) John Morton, Archbishop and Chancellor died of the plague, and thereby delivered England of a pestilence."

In 1503 died Sir Reginald Bray KG, former steward and indefatigable courier for his mistress Lady Margaret Beaufort, who became a notably hard collector of taxes during the reign of her son and, with John Morton, was specifically and particularly vilified by the Cornishmen. In his will he noted with gratitude that all his wealth and all he had achieved in life was entirely due to that great lady, the King's Mother. A year later, unsung and unmourned, Thomas, second Lord Stanley, first Earl of Derby also departed this life, Killer of Kings, trimmer, lickspittle, gone to his final accounting. His younger son, James, with his step-mother's backing, was to become Bishop of Ely, where he impressed only by his worldliness and lack of learning.

Henry Tudor passed to a better world on 22nd April 1508 aged 52 at his palace of Richmond. An avid collector of dues, taxes and fines - including one impost of £ 10,000 on his great general, the Earl of Oxford for a technical breach of an obscure regulation - he died the wealthiest of English monarchs, leaving in treasure alone, "most of it in secret places under his own key and keeping", £ 1,800,000. In today's terms, the sum in question would be defined as around three and a quarter *Billion* pounds. The penniless Welsh exile of Brittany and France, clinging to a remote, near-worthless claim to the throne of England, had indeed made good. He left one son, cast somewhat in the image of his maternal grandfather rather than that of the erstwhile heir of Cadwallader, who would become England's most married King, complete his father's work of eliminating the House of Plantagenet of York by beheading Margaret, Countess of Salisbury and daughter of George of Clarence in 1541, and destroy the Church to which his parent and grandmother had been so dedicated.

Margaret, Countess of Richmond and Derby, most tenacious of all Beauforts, outlived the son to whose success and succession her life had been dedicated. She died, aged 66, in June 1509 during the accession ceremonies of her grandson Henry VIII and was thus spared the anguish of seeing the consequences of her descendant's dedicated womanising. She may have had some prescience of what was to come, since it is said she wept profusely at the coronation. Her later years were dedicated to prayer and good works; she founded colleges, disbursed charity and was constantly - and painfully, due to her arthritic knee joints - at her devotions. Particularly notable was her concern for poorer undergraduates at Cambridge to many of whom she was "as a second mother". It was almost as though she was doing self-imposed penance for some unpardonable sin - but that, of course, would be unthinkable.

**Effigy of Cardinal Archbishop John Morton from his tomb
in the crypt of Canterbury Cathedral**

AUTHOR'S NOTES

This account of events during the last 20 years of the Fifteenth Century is based entirely on the same orthodox historical resources, which have been used by other writers down the ages to prove conclusions very different to those reached in "The Deceivers".

To avoid undue disturbance to the flow of the account, footnotes and all references to resource material have been avoided throughout the main body of the narrative, but, lest it be thought that this history is little more than a "factional" account of the events and characters it purports to portray, the sources from which the material for each chapter is drawn are detailed in the following pages, together with any necessary, explanatory comments.

One entirely fictional source which has been used throughout the book (excepting Chapters Three and Eight) to provide apposite chapter headings is the play Richard III by William Shakespeare. The author yields to none in his admiration of the Bard's abilities as a writer, but prefers to say nothing of his qualities as an historian, other than that he seems to have been seriously misled.

CHAPTER ONE

The death of Edward IV is very well documented and original accounts by Dominic Mancini/C.A.J. Armstrong, Commynes, Polydore Vergil and the Crowland Chronicler have come down through Gairdner, Ramsay, and, more latterly, through Paul Kendall. There is some speculation in various accounts as to whether or not Edward was in fact poisoned, with one writer in particular (R.E. Collins in John Dening's "Secret History") presenting a well-argued case pinpointing arsenic as the medium used and naming the guilty parties as Edward's Queen, Elizabeth Woodville, with the collusion of her son, Thomas Grey, Marquis of Dorset, and her brother, Sir Edward Woodville.

Their motive is alleged to be fear of losing their pre-eminence at Edward's court - and thereby their political power in the land - the solution to which would be to replace Edward with his son, who would have been little more than a front for his avaricious relatives. There is, undoubtedly, a case to be made out for the theory, which could repay deeper research. However, the cause of Edward's untimely death has little bearing on events following, which provide the main theme of this history, and the author has preferred to follow the orthodox view in this narrative. The "cause of death" listed here is drawn from a paper by Clifford Brewer F.R.C.S., entitled A Medical History of the Kings and Queens of England, lodged in the Athenaeum Library and for sight of which I am most indebted to David Hill of Ormskirk.

The accounts of the Battles of Barnet and Tewkesbury included in the chapter are largely rewritten from the author's military history of the Wars of the Roses, "The Hollow Crowns", for which Alfred H. Burne was an important source on tactics and manoeuvres. Burne is usually a reliable expert on locations of battles and the development of an action; he is sometimes less accurate on the personalities involved, for example, placing the Duke of Somerset alongside the Earl of Warwick in Lancaster's front at Barnet. A more unlikely juxtaposition than Edmund Beaufort and Richard Neville fighting side by side it is difficult to imagine. The more so, when it is remembered that Beaufort was in the West Country only one day later, welcoming the returning Queen Margaret of Anjou ashore at Weymouth.

It would be churlish to make too much of Burne's comparatively few shortcomings, since he surely stands alone as an interpreter of military events, particularly during the late Middle Ages. In all his work he makes good use of what he calls IMP: "Inherent Military Probability", to determine whether a battle could have been sited, or developed, along the lines indicated by classical historians. The present writer has followed him in this by developing, over very many years, psychological profiles of all the major characters appearing in "The Deceivers" which have been used to determine the most likely course of action any individual would have taken in particular circumstances. Thus, IPP: "Inherent Psychological Probability" has played a most important role in the researching and writing of this book.

CHAPTER TWO

The events and - importantly - their sequence, narrated in Chapter Two, are drawn very largely from Mancini/Armstrong's "Usurpation of Richard III" (Chaps. four and five) and supporting information unearthed by Paul Kendall and noted in his biography of Richard III.

The personae of the main participants depicted are drawn from long acquaintance with all the people involved through forty years and more of reading about them, their reported actions and their apparent effect on, and dealings with, their contemporaries. The avarice and obsessive social-climbing of the Woodvilles generally - and of Edward's Queen in particular - is amply demonstrated in every history of the period. The last, and perhaps most glaring example, being the fact that there was insufficient money in King Edward's treasury to meet his modest funeral expenses, despite Mancini's comment that "...the royal treasure, the weight of which was said to be immense..." and the sainted More's description of a wall being knocked down at Westminster Abbey to facilitate the transfer of part of Edward's hoard into the sanctuary.

Why the young Edward should have chosen such a family to be his counter-balance to the power of Warwick and the Nevilles is beyond reasonable comprehension. The only possible explanation seems to lie in Edward's life-long propensity for the pursuit of a pretty face and the fact that, despite his high estate, he never "enforced a woman" (Mancini). Combine this aspect of his personality with the worldly-wise shrewdness of the young widowed Elizabeth Grey, who would not yield her virtue outwith marriage "even when Edward placed a dagger at her throat" (Mancini again) and Edward's capture becomes explicable. And, having made his bed, Edward would certainly have lain in it; indeed, although he indulged his proclivity for "the chase" throughout his life, the number of offspring he produced with Elizabeth Woodville indicates clearly that she never totally lost her grasp on his "more basic instincts".

Henry Stafford, Duke of Buckingham is one of the shadowy characters of the period, but undoubtedly one of the key players. His enforced marriage when he was barely out of puberty to an older, "common" woman, Katherine Woodville, clearly affected his mind, some sources even hint at a mild insanity. Mancini comments on Buckingham's instant sympathy with Richard since both had suffered insults at the hands of the Queen's ignoble family: "he had his own reasons for detesting the queen's kin: for, when he was younger, he had been forced to marry the queen's sister, whom he had scorned to wed on account of her humble origin".

Buckingham's opinion of the Woodvilles would have led him to draw the worst possible conclusion as to their likely course of action following Edward's death and their continuation in power would have been unsafe for him, in light of his known attitude to the family, and not to be borne in terms of the increased distinction which would be claimed by this brood of commoners. Little wonder then at his leap from obscurity to Richard's side, almost before Edward's brother had been made aware of the scheming in London. Little wonder at his subsequent meteoric and bloody career under the guidance of vastly superior - and much more ruthless - intelligences.

CHAPTER THREE

The main biographical sources for John Morton are the Life of John Morton by R.I. Woodhouse (1895), Sir Thomas More's "Utopia", and an earlier biography (used as source-material by Woodhouse) by John Budden MA Oxon, Reader at Magdalen, died June 11th 1620 (related to the Morton family on his mother's side) who, 10 years prior to his death, had produced a manuscript extract from his biography, presumably at the request of Sir George Morton, another descendant of the Cardinal-Archbishop's family, to whom it is addressed. This last text has been preserved through its inclusion in the "Proceedings of the Dorset Natural History and Antiquarian Field Club, Vol II 1879, in which it was entitled: "A Biographical Sketch of Cardinal Morton communicated by the President."

Additional or confirmatory details have been drawn from Commines, the Paston Letters, the Reverend Lumby's edition of Bacon's "King Henry VII", the Reverend Moberly's "The Early Tudors" and, most illuminatingly, from Dean W.F. Hook's "Lives of the Archbishops of Canterbury". For example, Hook notes: prior to Edward's expedition to France "to regain his crown", he sent Morton on missions in 1474 to the Emperor and to the King of Hungary to concert a league with them against Louis. During the same year, Edward was raising finance for his expedition by the system of Benevolences of which, Hook says. "when we connect the high favour with Edward to which Morton had suddenly risen with the underhand modes of raising money, afterwards adopted by the servants of Henry VII, of whom Morton was one, we must suspect that the Master of the Rolls (John Morton) had some share in suggesting to the royal mind that plan of benevolences, at first so plausible and really so oppressive".

Later, writing of the settlement with Louis, Hook says Louis distributed a "largesse" of 16,000 crowns among Edward's officials, who were "not numerous... Rotherham, Archbishop of York, and John Morton, Master of the Rolls"are among the persons particularly named as having their share in this 'spoiling of the Egyptians'. Although Morton was munificent on great occasions "yet he was avaricious and grasping; he was, consequently, never a popular man". Hook goes on (somewhat contrarily) that Morton had the power of drawing the friendship of people connected with him and was "himself a kind, loyal, devoted friend, ever ready to assist and support all in whom his confidence was placed."

CHAPTER FOUR

The principal source of background material on Margaret Beaufort is "The King's Mother" by Michael Jones and Malcolm Underwood. Although - apparently - a minor player in the drama of the Wars of the Roses, the Lady Margaret's course through the main events can be discerned from many standard sources on the period (most listed above under Chapter One) with, perhaps, some allowance being made for understandable over-adulation on the part of Tudor Historians such as Vergil, Hall and Holinshed.

One particularly interesting point which emerges from closer study of the Lady's life was her regular residence at Deeping, ten miles from Crowland Abbey. Although the recorder of the Crowland Continuation has never been identified with any certainty, it is clear he must have had accommodation in the Abbey and one can speculate on his possible discourses with one of the great survivors of the whole period as part of the essential research required to produce the famous endpiece of this great History. If such a link is accepted as "probable" it would do much to explain the generally anti-Ricardian tone of the latter part of the Chronicle.

CHAPTER FIVE

Kendall, in his biography of Richard III, states "contemporary historical narrative (for the period May/June, 1483) is scanty and confused", and with this one can only agree. Clearly there was a great deal of politicking going on, new alliances were forming, old ones dissolving, Richard was building the framework essential to the continued peaceful governance of the realm and securing his own position as Lord Protector in accordance with Edward's wishes. Following Gairdner, Kendall agrees that the seeds of Hastings' break with Richard were sewn during this time and rooted in Lord William's discontent with "his share of power".

While agreeing with their basic premise, it seems to this writer that neither of these distinguished Historians has considered the likelihood that Hastings' "discontent" was due mainly to the pre-eminence given to the new, rising star, Buckingham. Nor do they give any weight to the idea that a skilled, manipulator like Morton, or an experienced plotter like Margaret Beaufort would have found the time and circumstances ideal for the quiet fomentation of internecine strife among the key supporters of the House of York, and themselves ideally positioned to take advantage of the opportunities offered.

CHAPTER SIX

The narrative of the plot against Hastings - ironically, perhaps - stems from the account of the famous meeting of Richard's Council (as related in Shakespeare's Richard III, Act III, Scene IV) of which Dean Hook says: "we have (the details) upon the highest authority, from Morton himself, who narrated it to Sir Thomas More, *if he did not himself pen the narrative*" (Author's italics). Even so, the Shakespearean version of events - presumably following closely the 'inside story' from Morton/More - makes no sense dramatically or otherwise.

A single minor example: according to the Bard, Ratcliff was among those present at the meeting when in fact he was 200 miles away nearing York where he was bearing the King's urgent plea for armed support. Again, characters are constantly entering and exiting the scene, the opening takes 21 lines of dialogue, Gloucester then enters (presumably full of his plans to make away with Hastings) joins in meaningless chat for a further 15 lines, including a request to Morton (who then exits) for some of the good strawberries from his Holborn garden, and exits with Buckingham. Morton re-enters, after four lines of monologue from Derby (Stanley), saying he has sent for the desired fruit and Gloucester and Buckingham re-enter nine lines later still, with Richard going immediately into his "witchcraft" accusation, ending with instructions to Lovell, and (the absent) Ratcliff to see to Hastings' execution.

Dramatic nonsense, with half a dozen exits, entrances, re-entrances and re-exits by the major players within 80 lines of script. But, the account of the meeting on which the scene is based was provided by an eye-witness and the fundamentals have a certain ring of truth. There is no doubt that Richard and Buckingham had prepared drastic counteraction, nor that it took Hastings, and some of the others completely by surprise. The incident of the strawberries makes no contribution to the dramatic progress of the scene and is so bizarre that one must conclude it actually happened, but the request cannot have been made as a casual aside in an atmosphere so fraught with tension by either of the main players. It seems reasonable to conclude, therefore, that it was a pre-arranged signal to Morton and, as such, would not have come from Richard, who had no close relationship with the Bishop of Ely. The only logical alternative is that the signal was from Hastings to Morton and that the following account of events - including the accusations of Jane Shore's and the Queen's witchcraft which had famously withered Richard's arm - was heavily doctored by the one man who could have issued such a slanted report in the sure and certain hope of its credibility in the minds of the eventual, post-Plantagenet audience.

For the build-up to the Tower-meeting scene, there are ample sources in Mancini, More and Vergil as to the meetings which took place and Gairdner states his firm belief that Hastings was conspiring with others to secure the person of Edward V. The time-scale of the various events covered is entirely accurate, there is ample evidence of the plotting with the Woodville faction via the Queen, and there can be no doubt that Margaret Beaufort, although using her physician for much of her communication with the Sanctuary, must have at least initiated the negotiations in personal visits, to assure Edward's widow of the authenticity of the plotting and of the power that lay behind it.

In brief, this revised account of the Hastings' Plot develops logically from authenticated reports of writers who were hardly Ricardian sympathisers and the reader is left to judge whether or not it provides a more credible recital of the events which took place than versions supplied by previous commentators.

CHAPTER SEVEN

Apart from Mancini, who left England shortly after the coronation, there are few contemporary sources on developments during the period covered. Students must rely particularly on "The Usurpation of Richard III" therefore, together with the notes added by C. A. J. Armstrong, and on the digging by Paul Kendall through a vast variety of obscure tracts, the results of which are admirably detailed in that author's "Richard III" (1955).

CHAPTER EIGHT

The chronology and basic facts on which this Chapter is based are covered in many of the histories which have been written about the period. The only - and admittedly critical - material for which there is no written evidential background is the clandestine correspondence between Morton and Margaret Beaufort. Clearly, however, the two principal players in the plot must have kept in close touch and Reginald Bray would be the obvious courier in light of his life-long dedication to Margaret Beaufort before and after the events described in this book, and his following attachment to Morton and employment in the zealous application of 'Morton's Fork'.

The lack of written evidence of what passed between the two stars of this drama is regrettable - but hardly surprising in view of what the contents must have been. Detractors of Richard III have never allowed their lack of clear, indisputable written material from the actual period "to get in the way of a good story" and have invented "facts" where necessary to further their argument. All students of the period, for example, will be unhappily familiar with the argument that rumours said to be current during the reign of Henry VIII, forty years and more later, *"must therefore have been circulating equally"* (Author's italics) during the reign of Richard and people who can believe that should equally be prepared to accept this writer's imagining of the contents of letters between Beaufort and Morton, all of which are entirely in accordance with the principles of IPP, referred to above, and with the basic motivation of the characters concerned.

CHAPTER NINE

The last recorded meeting between Buckingham and Richard was at Gloucester during the Royal Progress. Although the Tudor Historians: Vergil and More suggest that Buckingham accompanied the King throughout the tour, the very detailed research done by Kendall makes clear that Henry Stafford was not with the Royal party during the first weeks of the tour, but joined - briefly - at Gloucester and went on immediately to Brecknock. The two never met again, and within days of their last encounter, Buckingham had commenced detailed planning for his rebellion.

Although there is - again - a lack of detailed, contemporary commentary on the actions of principal characters, their whereabouts are known with certainty and, given the tidings Buckingham brought to Richard and his certain reception of such news, there can be little question of the outcome of their interview. Nor of the palpable lie developed by Hall, the Tudor Historian in his account of the supposed accidental meeting between Buckingham and his aunt, Margaret Beaufort, after the parting of the ways in Gloucester, in which she convinces the Duke to bend all his efforts to support the rightful claim of her son to the throne. (Followed also by Woodhouse in his Life of John Morton.) As has been said before, a likely story. Both Hall and Vergil, however, join in describing Buckingham's "outrage" at his supposed treatment by Richard during their talk, and Vergil goes on to describe Buckingham's following discussion with Morton, "who enthusiastically set about putting (the plan for rebellion) into operation by sending word to the Countess of Richmond in London".

Vergil describes Margaret Beaufort's enthusiastic reception of the news, since she had "already persuaded Queen Elizabeth to give her support to such a rebellion" and had won further assurances of support from gentlemen such as Richard Guilford and John Cheyney. Kendall doubts Vergil's accuracy on the grounds that this account would give Margaret Beaufort too prominent a role in the planning of the insurrection and thus invalidate the known involvement of the Woodville faction. This writer begs to differ; much of Vergil's (and Hall's) writing is obvious fiction, but some is clearly developed from information supplied by "The King's Mother" and, here and there amid the misdirection, emerge accidental nuggets of pure truth. Similarly, it is possible to wonder whether Shakespeare's version of Buckingham's words after parting from Richard (See Chapter heading) had not been passed, verbatim, to the Bard from a knowledgeable source, for they have the ring of truth about them.

CHAPTER TEN

Richard's itinerary through England and his diplomatic activities during his tour are drawn from various sources including the Harleian MS 433, Vergil, York Records, Rous, and the Paston Letters and the admirable summary of much of this data in Kendall.

Buckingham's rebellion is not well documented apart from coverage in the Crowland Continuation and in Vergil, both of which are drawn on by Gairdner for his Henry VII (1889). Additional references to Morton's movements are contained in Budden's Biographical Sketch (republished 1879).

CHAPTER ELEVEN

The principal sources for Henry Tudor's landing in Wales, his march through that country and into England, and his several encounters with the Stanleys are the Crowland Chronicle, Vergil, Hall, Stowe and, more latterly, Gairdner and the comparatively modern summaries of Kendall, and A.H. Burne in his Battlefields of England (1950).

CHAPTER TWELVE

The Battle of Bosworth is well-documented by all the Tudor Historians and the Crowland Chronicle, by Gairdner, Oman and Ramsay and, of course, by Burne, who properly acknowledges the debt of all later writers to the work done by Hutton and his editor, Nichols, in the early 19th Century. All of the material has been re-sifted by Burne and this writer has largely followed his account, in particular as to Richard's dispositions and the (related) movements of the two, separate forces of the Stanleys. Why Ramsay would assume they were united on one side only of the main action is difficult to comprehend. Similarly, the reasons for Burne's own apparent problems in rationalising Oxford's march across the front of Richard's army, and the lack of an immediate flank assault by Richard, are obscure. Given the (forced) disposition of his own army, Richard had no option but to await events.

This new account of the Battle of Bosworth is an extended version of the writer's original description in his military history of the Wars of the Roses, "The Hollow Crowns" and the "3-D" battlemap included here has also been taken from the earlier History to clarify the action to readers of this book

One final point: Burne's account, as usual, makes much use of IMP to justify his placings of the various forces involved and their movements during the battle. The writer has made similar use of IPP in describing the involvement in the fight (or lack of it) of Henry Tudor and the deeds of Lord Stanley. Any readers who may prefer the more heroic version provided by Shakespeare, amongst others, are recommended to spend time looking at the portraits of the former (and remembering that these must be flattering likenesses) and rechecking the record of the latter.

CHAPTER THIRTEEN

The course of events immediately after Bosworth are well-documented in Bacon's Life of Henry VII, illuminated subsequently by Gairdner, and in Woodhouse's Life of Morton. All these sources have been drawn on freely to provide essential chronological and locational background information for the principal characters in the narrative. Their varying motivations have been deduced by the writer from their recorded actions and their established traits of character.

CHAPTER FOURTEEN

The rebellion centred on Lambert Simnel is covered in detail by Gairdner and, particularly, in Bacon's Henry VII, which also gives an account of Stoke Field, the events leading up to the Battle, and its aftermath. Both these writers depend largely on Vergil, who seems to have been the main authority in all following centuries and who may well have had the advantage of recording the recollections of some of the leading persons involved on the Tudor side.

The main source for the battle is Burne who draws heavily on the classical first-hand account by Henry Tudor's Herald as subsequently related by Richard Brooke in his "Visits to Fields of Battle in England" (1857). Burne uses IMP to settle controversy over the movements of the armies prior to the engagement and provides the definitive, modern account of the battle, though with the usual minuscule and confusing map. He also gets his facts somewhat mixed while developing his narrative, in referring to the "gruesome thoughts" evoked in the mind of the Earl of Lincoln when crossing the old battlefield of Towton on his march south, "for on that field had perished his grandfather, Richard Duke of York, claimant to the throne." York was, in fact, killed by Lord Clifford after his defeat at Wakefield, three months prior to England's bloodiest day at Towton and his head decorated the Micklegate Bar at York while his son, Edward IV, was winning what some regard as his greatest victory.

Events following the battle are well-documented in Bacon and Vergil. There is some confusion as to the exact time when Elizabeth Woodville's part in the Simnel Plot became clear, but none about her banishment to the Bermondsey Nunnery where she was to stay for the last four years of her life. Bacon's final commentary on this event is revealing: "...she (was) upon dark and unknown reasons, and no less strange pretences, precipitated and banished the world into a nunnery; *where it was almost thought dangerous to visit her, or see her*; and where not long after she ended her life..." (Author's italics) The account of the discussion between Henry VII, his mother and John Morton in this narrative makes Bacon's otherwise strange - and, clearly, puzzled - comments a perfectly logical and simple statement of fact.

CHAPTER FIFTEEN

Henry VII's campaign in France and the preparations therefor are covered in Vergil, the Crowland Chronicle's Third Continuation, Gairdner and Bacon. The inception of Morton's Fork, as it has come to be known, stemmed from this second series of Benevolences and is thereby forever laid at the door of Henry Tudor. To be fair, however, as Dean Hook comments, it is most probable that Morton (and Bray) were merely reviving a revenue-raising measure that had been found most useful by Edward IV. It is doubtful though that Henry was able to mitigate the offence felt by many of the cheerful givers in the same way his father-in-law had, by offering a kiss to the more generous lady donors. If he did, the occasions have not been recorded.

The death of Northumberland while trying to collect the tax for his new master is well documented, as is the fine levied on his estate to purge Henry Percy's failure to collect the King's dues from his north Yorkshire subjects. The "campaign" in France is covered by most of the sources referred to, the accounts used are those of Gairdner and Bacon, though both seem to give more importance to the prior machinations of Spain and the Emperor, in which Henry involved himself. Certainly, Henry was anxious to develop friendlier relations with Spain, as witness the eventual betrothal of his elder son to Catherine of Aragon, but it is equally likely that the operations of his allies, which petered out before the English landing, were merely a useful camouflage for Henry Tudor's (and John Morton's) main purpose: the amplification of the treasure chest of the King of England.

The same two sources provide the background to the introduction of the Perkin Warbeck affair and the involvement of Sir William Stanley.

CHAPTER SIXTEEN

Gairdner and Bacon again provide the main source material, though much of this chapter is based on the application of IPP to actual events. Warbeck's attempt on the English throne is well-documented by both writers drawing largely on Vergil, who was followed by the other Tudor Historians.

It was a much more threatening episode than it appears today, 500 years on, and given Henry Tudor's nervous disposition, the reasonable assumption - to put it no more strongly - that Warbeck could well have been a son of Edward IV (who would certainly not have let a few months in Burgundian exile interfere with his normal proclivity for dalliance with the fairer sex), the unresponsive attitude of Europe's rulers to Henry's pleas for support, and the final blow of Warbeck's alliance with the Scots, there can be little doubt that Henry VII, Margaret Beaufort and John Morton needed to make some form of devastating response to Warbeck's claims.

There is no exact timing of the first emergence of reports of the death of Edward IV's sons. Effectively, they disappeared from view after their exclusion from the succession and being little known to the people of England were quickly forgotten. Henry Tudor made no statement on the boys' deaths when he landed at Milford Haven, nor following his victory at Bosworth. The root of all historical lore on the alleged murder of the Princes by Richard III is the biography by Thomas More, supported in the following History by Vergil, which are clearly based on contemporary, eye-witness reports and which, in turn, could only have come from one source.

It seems most probable to this writer that the popular fiction of Richard III's involvement in the murder of his nephews was initiated at the time, and for the reasons stated here, and was subsequently elaborated and pre-dated by following historians using Morton's papers - knowingly or not - as the basis for their own works.

EPILOGUE

The timing and circumstances of the deaths of the main characters in this history are taken from the sources listed previously. The opinions are the writer's own.

ACKNOWLEDGEMENTS

It would be impossible to acknowledge properly here, the extent and depth of my indebtedness to so many kind people – old friends and new – who have encouraged me in my efforts to prove, once and for all, Richard III's innocence of the murder of his nephews, "The Princes in the Tower". I believe each of them will know whether they are included in my heartfelt thanks to all of them, and I hope they will feel the contents of this book to be sufficient reward for their help.

On grounds of practical support, however, I can – and must – give specific and most sincere thanks to a number of people who have helped me along the way, in particular (and in order of approach):

Carolyn Hammond, Librarian of the Richard III Society, who advised me on the best sources, supplied every book I requested "instanter", and tried – unsuccessfully – to warn me off Sir George Buck (you were right, dear lady).

Christine Symonds, who fills the same role in my own Yorkshire Branch of the Society, with equal skill, expediton and forbearance, and who guards a veritable treasurehouse of knowledge on the Wars of the Roses, deserving much greater use by Branch members;

Geoffrey Wheeler, who controls Press Records and Exhibitions and the Tape Library of the Society, and whose personal knowledge of "matters illustrative" in relation to the Wars of the Roses is incredibly wide and exceeded only by his willingness to help those less fortunate;

The Society of Antiquaries of London for permission to use the Royal portraits from their marvellous collection, and their Assistant Librarian, Adrian James, whose prompt and courteous way with enquiries is helpful in the extreme.

To all of you my thanks - I hope you will think that "The Deceivers" was worth the trouble.

Index

Also available from Baildon Books

Geoffrey Richardson's

THE HOLLOW CROWNS

For the first time – all major battles of the Wars of the Roses
in detail and in one volume.

From the fields and gardens by St Albans on an early Summer's day in 1455, to the death of the last Plantagenet King of England, alone, betrayed and hopelessly mired in marshland below Bosworth's Ambion Hill, the reader is swept along through three decades of English History.

Encountering along the way: the hapless Henry VI, pathetic son of the victor of Agincourt; Margaret of Anjou, Henry's Queen and Lancaster's champion for 20 years; Richard Neville, fabled Kingmaker Warwick, who – the story shows – has enjoyed a greater reputation in history than his deeds warranted; the giant Edward IV, England's greatest Warrior-King, and Richard, his youngest brother, arguably the last true monarch of England and almost certainly the worst-slandered.

This all-new account of the bloodiest 30 years in English History has been termed: "History made easy - and interesting!" Written in a fresh narrative style, with full-page, "3D" Battlemaps of all eleven major conflicts and portraits of the principal participants (including line-drawings of Warwick and Margaret of Anjou developed from computer-enhanced sources) THE HOLLOW CROWNS" puts the story back into History.

ISBN 0 9527621 0 2

AND...

Geoffrey Richardson's

"THE LORDLY ONES"

The original History of the Neville family, from its beginnings in the reign of King John, to its effective end in the swirling mists of Barnet on Easter Day, 1471.

From their great Keep at Middleham and their other northern fortresses at Barnard, Sheriff Hutton, Carlisle and Richmond, the Nevilles spread their power throughout England, notably through Richard Neville, Earl of Warwick, who made another power-base at Warwick Castle and sought to rule all the land by the making and unmaking of Kings.

The saga of his efforts - and his failure - is an important element in this history, but the author, in his inimitable, easy-read style, shows that there was much more to the history of the Nevilles than the often-told story of "Warwick the Kingmaker". Among "The Lordly Ones" we meet Ralph Neville, Lord of Raby, victor over the Scots at Nevilles Cross; and another Ralph, first Earl of Westmorland, and most uxorious of all this well-married family, with his brood of 23 children. Joan Beaufort, Ralph's second wife, who brought the blood-royal into the family, with fatal consequences. Cecily Neville, Ralph's youngest, fairest, star-crossed daughter, the Rose of Raby, wife to a would-be King, mother to two more, and Great Grand-dam to the usurping line of Tudors - her greatest tragedy would be to outlive nearly all her line.

And tragedy a-plenty among the other Nevilles: John, Marquis Montagu, the faithful Yorkist, killed fighting for the wrong side. His son George, a royal Duke, heir to the throne of England, who died a pauper dependant on his cousin's charity. And the two daughters of the Kingmaker, who married splendidly - but not wisely - and died young. Not untypically, for death - early and sudden - was the constant attendant of the Lordly Ones, the Nevilles, and of most of those who came close to them.

ISBN 09527621 2 9

Geoffrey Richardson's

THE POPINJAYS

Another first from the writer who believes in "putting the story back into History": the first-ever History of the Woodvilles, the upstart nobodies, whose only attributes were good-looks, ambition and persistence, but who were to mingle their blood-line with those of the greatest families in the land.

Their rise to greatness sprang from the marriage between Richard Woodville, "the handsomest man in England" and Jacquetta of Luxembourg, Duchess of Bedford, the fair, passionate descendant of Melusine the Water-witch. Widowed at nineteen, she found quick consolation in the charms of her late husband's dashing young Lieutenant. The romance between these young lovers started in overly-hasty wedlock, which cost the wealthy bride dearly in monetary terms. As time went by, it would levy an even higher charge on her adopted country in blood and treasure - but this unsuitable, ill fated coupling endured for more than 30 of the most troublous years in England's history.

The Wars of the Roses as they were named, centuries later, by Sir Walter Scott, followed closely on the ending of the Hundred Years War. The dream of French Empire was gone. The land was filled with nobles and soldiers who had spent their entire lives winning fame and fortune through armed prowess. The King was weak, and his haughty, French Queen, closely allied with a bastard sprig of her husband's kin, envied, suspected, and eventually came to hate a resurgent royal line with powerful allies and a better claim to the crown than its feeble wearer.

Thus did Lancaster and York, Beauforts and Nevilles come to clash in the internecine conflict which convulsed England for three decades, killed more than half of the landed aristocracy and, at the last, brought to ruin the royal house of Plantagenet which had ruled England - and much of France - for more than three hundred years.

And through it all, the Woodvilles managed to thrive, loyal first to one side then the other, gaining, losing, but always surviving. Their tendrils - and their fortunes - intertwined inseparably with the great ones of the land. Not brave in battle, not skilful in the Council Chamber, their ambition always outrunning their abilities and yet, the Woodvilles survived into a new Century, into the New Age and the dire cost of their durability was paid in large measure by those to whom they had attached themselves.

ISBN 09527621 3 7

"THE HOLLOW CROWNS"

"...it is in The Hollow Crowns' vivid descriptions of the wars' 11 major battles that Richardson shows his considerable ability as a researcher and writer. He provides easily understandable explanations of the courses of the battles themselves, displaying an expert knowledge of such decisive factors as topography, weather conditions and weaponry. In addition Richardson presents in an entertaining and comprehensible manner, the complex and highly fluid relationships between the numerous characters involved....As an alternative view of a well-known and turbulent time, The Hollow Crowns is highly recommended to anyone interested in medieval warfare, the history of England, or the foibles of royalty." (MILITARY HISTORY MAGAZINE.)

"THE DECEIVERS"

"...The author, who has been fascinated by history since he was a schoolboy has treated the book as an enthralling detective story... making the subject interesting and entertaining...He makes a persuasive case for Richard III and pins the blame [for the Princes' murder] on the plotting of three 15th century schemers...[He says] I am writing about events that happened 500 years ago, but people were driven then by the same things that drive them now - ambition, pride and desire for power..." (EVENING COURIER)

"THE LORDLY ONES"

"...The pages of The Lordly Ones are full of sex, power and dark deeds in high places, but don't be confused. It is not a modern-day blockbuster. The writer has taken a spin back through the centuries to unearth the story of one of England's most powerful family dynasties and more than 300 years of the Neville family have been retraced in vivid style. The Bradford-based author was asked by English Heritage to write the story of the Nevilles and their Area Director, Sue Constantine said "The book fills an important gap in the story of Middleham Castle and indeed English History generally..." (NORTHERN ECHO)